D1119082

Frances Tenenbaum, Series Editor

HOUGHTON MIFFLIN COMPANY
Boston • New York   2000

Cold Climate Gardening

How to select and grow the best vegetables
and ornamental plants for the North

REBECCA ATWATER BRICCETTI

Taylor's Guide and *Taylor's Weekend Gardening Guides* are registered trademarks of
Houghton Mifflin Company.

Library of Congress Cataloging-in-Publication Data

Briccetti, Rebecca W. Atwater.
Cold climate gardening / Rebecca Atwater Bricetti.
        p.   cm. — (Taylor's weekend gardening guides)
      Includes bibliographical references (p.   ) and index.
        ISBN 0-395-86044-X
        1. Gardening — Snowbelt States. I. Title. II. Series.
SB453.2.S58B75 2000
635.9'52—dc21   99-28989

Printed in the United States of America

WCT 10 9 8 7 6 5 4 3 2 1

Book design by Deborah Fillion
Cover photograph © by Rick Mastelli

CONTENTS

Gardening in a cold climate offers challenges: a shorter growing season, less-than-nurturing conditions, a seemingly more modest palette of plants, slower rates of growth, and the unexpectedly early (or late) killing frost. When conversation turns to gardening in colder climates, someone is always eager to point out brightly, "Oh, but some plants *prefer* cooler growing conditions." That is quite true, and it's very nice, as far as it takes you. Still, that is hardly the silver lining of the situation. The fact is that every location has its limitations, and it pays to try to understand the limitations of yours. Gardening in USDA Zones 3, 4, and 5 is considerably different than it is in, say, Virginia, which is mostly in Zone 7. It calls for thoughtful plant selection and attentiveness to the vagaries of the weather. Happily, with some planning for the growing season ahead, you can enjoy and grow well many of the plants you like best, and help them flourish in spite of almost anything nature can throw their way. Thanks to the tireless work of plant breeders, horticulturists, and propagators, selected varieties of plants have been bred to thrive in colder climates, and many of these are recommended in the pages that follow.

In a splendid meadow planting, the orange-red of these Oriental poppies (Papaver orientale) virtually vibrates among the emerald foliage and white spires of gas plant (Dictamnus albus). Soft tones ranging from pale pink through magenta to lavender are sprinkled here and there across the canvas.

Chapter 1
Cold
Considerations

Anyone looking for plants to grow in a cold-winter climate is interested in hardiness. In theory, hardiness is the degree of cold a plant can survive. But it isn't simply a plant's cold-hardiness that determines whether it will pull through harsh weather, though from a plant's point of view, that is where it starts. Other factors affect survival, and gardeners can do quite a bit to increase the odds. Still, every plant seems to have an innate point of cold-hardiness. A plant is able to tolerate the greatest degree of cold if it has had the opportunity to acclimate itself to the environmental changes accompanied by the decreasing temperatures and day length in autumn. Keep in mind that cold-hardiness is gauged under ideal conditions that allow a plant to prepare itself in timely fashion for the cold—the amount of sun, moisture, and nutrients it prefers, the happy absence of disease and pests, and so forth.

Those plants that are able to survive cold temperatures prepare for the cold ("acclimate"). Then, cued by warmer temperatures and longer days, they prepare for spring ("deacclimate"). A plant that has been unable to prepare itself sufficiently may be injured or killed by cold, whether it be the cold at winter's

Beauty often lies in such details as the hoarfrost that defines the margins of these leaves of Italian parsley.

onset or a revisit of cold weather after temperatures begin to rise in spring. In preparation for freezing temperatures, some of the water in plant cells is moved out into the spaces *between* the cells; there the water can expand, as water does when it freezes, without exploding and killing the cells. If surprised by unexpected cold—a dip, frost, snap, or bitter freeze—plants may suffer. They may experience tissue or root damage here or there, leaf burn, dieback, or any of these so seriously that they expire. An abrupt drop in temperature can kill, even if the plant has withstood that degree of cold before.

Many factors affect the survival of a plant. Robust plants are best able to withstand the challenges. A plant troubled by pests or disease is likely to acclimate or deacclimate less well. The same is true of a plant that gets too much or too little sun, too much or too little moisture, too much wind or too little air circulation, or one that endures indifferent cultural care. See that your perennial plants get what they need; that's the first and most important step in winter protection.

Plants die of cold when their cells freeze, and they die of thirst if they need to take up moisture in the soil but can't because it is frozen. Root-killing temperatures are generally in the range of 14° to 19°F, so when we look at the huge percentage of winter survivors, we can appreciate what a good insulator soil is. Some people build gardens entirely of plants that survive by dint of their own efforts; the plants aren't coddled in the least. I'm willing to bet that most gardeners, though, find at least *some* other plants alluring enough that they are pleased to give them some help in seeing the cold weather through in good shape. There's a happy medium for every gardener that lies somewhere between leaving all the plants on their own and fussing over lots of them. When you think about adding a new plant to your garden, it's reasonable to consider whether you can manage to provide additional care if it's needed.

HEDGE YOUR BETS

To garden is to gamble. When you set out tender plants in mid-May, you are gambling there won't be a late-spring frost. Still, as with other games of chance, when you gamble with plants you can hedge your bets. To give your plants the best possible odds, you should protect them from the worst of the cold temperatures and drying winds.

Mulch

Consider the threat of frost heaves. Frost heaves occur when the soil freezes, thaws, and then freezes again, pushing roots up and sometimes out of the soil; the exposed root tissue is injured or killed by the cold. Snow is a good insulator, and that's why gardeners in cold climates hope for thick and consistent snow cover that stays all through the winter. It protects plant growth above ground, and it lessens the likelihood of frost heaves.

Of course, storybook snow cover is never guaranteed. It's possible to reduce the potential for damage from frost heaves: When you're sure the ground has frozen, lay on a good layer of mulch, at least 2 to 3 inches thick. You can use compost with a layer of straw on top, or shredded leaves (whole leaves form a mat that keeps water from reaching the plants). You must remove the winter mulch come spring, when the plants begin to grow. Leaving mulch on too long into spring delays the plants' growth. It should be removed from around roses (if used; see page 93) as soon as you observe swollen buds, probably sometime in early April. Other recommended mulches for trees and shrubs include pine needles or decomposed pine bark (not hardwood bark, which can promote molds and fungus), to a maximum depth of 4 inches. Don't pack mulch right up against the trunk of the tree. For perennials, pine needles and pine boughs are recommended.

Protecting Plants from Wind

Adequate rainfall isn't guaranteed, and many plants will suffer if forced to enter winter under droughty conditions. Like mulching, providing sufficient water is a form of insurance. And because many plants lose moisture to evaporation through their leaves, strong winds can be severely drying. A plant that loses critical moisture to wind will not be able to replace that moisture if the water in the soil is frozen. Buildings, walls, various other structures and even other plants can offer shelter from the wind. A hedge (provided it doesn't mind the wind itself) or shelterbelt of trees and shrubs can modify forceful winds. And that's just what's wanted, to modify rather than block the wind. Because a solid, impermeable barrier may channel wind in another direction with even greater force, or allow the windbreak to be blown over, a good windbreak allows some of the wind to pass through; the effect is gentling, not blocking. Windbreak fences are commercially available, and homemade burlap screens cut down on wind veloc-

(Above) Zone-up, which protects an individual plant or a tightly spaced grouping, is said to warm the environment around the plant by the equivalent of a hardiness zone. (Right) These snap-together panels help reduce the damage of dessication.

ity too. Windbreak netting (also called windbreak "cloth") can be stretched between poles or posts, zigzag fashion so it's not broadside to prevailing winds; this netting is designed to permit some wind to pass through, as well as moisture and light.

Plants can be individually sheltered, or protected in communities. Burlap is often used to wrap a plant that needs protection, and the burlap coat can be stuffed with leaves for insulation. Burlap allows good air circulation as it protects the plant from damage by the weight of ice and snow, from the wind's drying effect, from killing frost, and from too much sun. Some gardeners bundle the plant in burlap and wrap the package with sturdy garden twine. Others erect a frame of stakes or poles to support the burlap and hold it away from the sides and top of the plant.

There are fancier, prefab "plant wraps": Zone-up, described as a "closed-cell foam blanket … that insulates from sunscald, windburn, and cold," is said to warm the plant's immediate environment by one hardiness zone. It resembles a cover for patio furniture. Snap-together, plastic modular panels can be linked as the gardener requires to fashion a bulwark to surround a plant. (If these protective devices will be easily seen from indoors, remember you will be looking at them for months.) Windbreak cloth or wire mesh filled with leaves, peat moss, and even newspaper have been used, too. And, when it comes to roses, catalogs and garden stores usually offer numerous winter protection structures from which to choose (see page 95). For teepees and sawhorses to limit ice and snow damage to shrubby plants, see chapter 8. When milder weather arrives, it is important to unwrap protected plants with care; overcast weather is best for this, for sunlight at full strength can be a shock.

Covers and Tunnels

Row covers and their larger incarnation, garden tunnels, protect plant communities. These temporary structures are usually erected to protect plants until there is no longer any chance of frost, or the plants outgrow them; then they are dismantled and stored for use the following year (they may last several years). They consist of light-transmissible fabric, usually supported by metal hoops; when the fabric is draped directly over the growing plants, it is called a floating row cover or, if of a heavier gauge, a garden blanket. Leave the fabric loose so plants can push it up as they grow. Many row-cover fabrics let water through.

Protecting Container Plants

Plants in containers are especially susceptible to cold. A plant that might be expected to survive the winter nicely out in the garden faces dire circumstances when it lives in a pot, for pots aren't insulated by surrounding soil. Not only is the soil terribly cold, but it freezes and thaws repeatedly, which is much worse than freezing just once. To protect a container-grown plant too large (or temperamental) to bring indoors for the winter: Loosely insulate the soil surface and the spaces between branches with dry straw or lots of dry leaves. Then wrap the container, from under the bottom to up and over the plant, with an insulating material such as burlap or shade cloth. Secure the wrap enough so you can keep filling this "coat," then tie it closed with twine. It is critical that the "stuffing" never be allowed to get wet, and if there is any chance of that, protect the top of the bundle with a piece of heavy plastic. In the case of the largest containers or tall plants, it is helpful to wrap a sort of cage of wire fencing (such as chicken wire) around the pot, up at least as high as the plant reaches. This fashions a sort of tube that is easily filled with stuffing, then covered with burlap.

A row cover protects from some degree of frost, keeping the plants warmer so they grow and yield crops better. Row covers are also an extremely effective and nontoxic insect deterrent. You can think of putting covers in place as the last step in planting.

Do install hoops to support the more fragile fabrics above crops that might otherwise poke holes, such as the pointy tips of peppers. Some fabrics trap a great deal of radiant heat, and it's important to watch that plants aren't dangerously overheated on very sunny, warm days. Others raise temperatures by no more than 4°F during the daytime; they were developed to protect heat-sensitive crops from insects. Another row-cover material is clear plastic (with slits for wind tolerance), to maximize light and wind protection. Row-cover and blanket fabrics range from 50 to 85 percent light transmissible.

The "garden tunnel" is essentially a giant row cover, supported by hoops about 5 feet tall. The draping fabrics used for tunnels may be insulating, insect-deterring, or shading (to deter bolting).

Winterburn and Sunscald

If exposed to desiccating winds, some plants can be seriously damaged by winterburn. Broad-leaved evergreens—hollies, leucothoes, mahonias, mountain laurels, and rhododendrons—lose quite a bit of moisture through their foliage as a matter of course during winter. When they are unable to replenish that moisture because the ground about their roots is frozen, and drying, harsh winds compound the water loss, they first show evidence of winterburn—brown, dead foliage—in May or June. Rhododendrons curl their leaves to reduce water loss, evergreens turn an unhealthy bronze when they lose moisture. Liquid latex antidesiccant sprays are thought to reduce evaporation from leaf surfaces by about 80 percent. Among these products are Wilt-Pruf, Stop-Wilt, Foli-gard, D-Wax and Plant-cote, and there are others. Apply antidesiccant at temperatures of 50°F or higher (in southern New Hampshire, there's usually a period of warmer weather sometime in November, or a January thaw). Follow the manufacturer's directions, though, for this product is *not* a universal garden spray for every plant.

Another challenge the cold-climate gardener is apt to face, even if not very often (unless you keep an orchard), is sunscald. Sunscald tends to affect thin-barked trees such as mountain ash, some maples, apple and peach, and occasionally some vegetables (bell peppers, for example; it results in watery blisters,

Once supporting hoops are set in place, it's a simple matter to secure light-transmissible fabric over them to fashion a convenient row cover.

so harvest the fruit immediately). Our local extension expert says that he confidently diagnoses sunscald injuries described to him over the telephone as occurring on the southwestern exposure of a young, thin-barked tree — the circumstances are that particular. Sunscald results where late-afternoon sun heats a portion of a plant to as much at 70°F, and then nighttime temperatures plunge to something in the neighborhood of -10°F. This kills the conductive tissue.

Susceptible vegetable crops can be covered for overnight protection, but trees call for different measures. To protect young, thin-barked trees, apply a tree wrap around Thanksgiving. Commercial tree wraps are available, usually in the form of stretchy tape. Aluminum foil will work in a pinch. A different preventive measure is to dilute latex interior paint and apply it to the tree trunk. Use white paint, which reflects sunlight. It will gradually wear off the tree. Remove the wrap in spring; if the trunk has split, follow the directions of a good tree manual to clean out the wound with a knife, then let it heal into

On sunny—and even on partly sunny—days, it is wise to check that plants under hot caps, cloches, and their kin don't become dangerously overheated.

a sort of elliptical scar. The risk of sunscald is a compelling reason for not pruning in late autumn, for such pruning can remove protective cover and expose vulnerable plant tissues. Yews, for example, pruned too late in the year may become quite bronzy and experience considerable dieback. Also, you can lose bark to cold; it freezes and pulls away from the tree.

THE TRANSITION FROM INDOORS TO OUT

Wherever they live, gardeners may need—or want—to start some of their plants from seed. Plants started indoors must be permitted to acclimate to the conditions of growing outdoors gradually; otherwise, the shock can kill them. This period of transition is called hardening off. It will take tender plants such as tomatoes as long as two weeks to make the transition.

At first, you must protect new seedlings from direct sun as well as from cold temperatures and chilling winds. Set them in a shady spot, near the warmth of a wall if possible. Leave them there for an hour or so a day for the first few days, bringing them back indoors when their time is up. If the weather continues to be mild, you can gradually increase their exposure daily after that. The second week, move them to a location that gets a bit more sun — dappled shade is good — and expose them for about an hour in the morning and late afternoon to full sun. When the seedlings have spent a good portion of each day outdoors, you can leave them out overnight. Pay attention to forecasts for overnight temperatures; this is one of the times a garden blanket is handy. If your work means you can't potter around your young plants while they're hardening off (isn't that the case for most of us?), you may need to enlist the help of a friend or neighbor.

A cold frame makes hardening off a much less high-maintenance job. If you have the luxury of a cold frame (see page 16): Open the vents slightly during the day, and shade the seedlings lightly; at night, you will want to bring the young plants back indoors to their accustomed spot. After a few days, you can leave them in the cold frame overnight, but close the top to keep the day's warmth inside. Bit by bit, increase the sun exposure and open the cold frame to the circulation of outdoor air.

Some nursery-grown seedlings may also benefit from a gradual transition to the garden. Give them a couple of days to get up to speed before planting them out. Check your plants for sufficient moisture at least daily when hardening off. The humidity of a seedling's environment shouldn't be changed any more abruptly than its temperature. You'll want to "harden off" for moisture, too, in the case of seedlings raised under plastic in very moist situations. Don't just whip the covering from the plants one day. Vent the plastic by raising it at one side a bit, or by poking a few small holes in it. Wait a couple of days, then vent some more, proceeding gradually until the humidity about the seedling and in the surrounding atmosphere are comparable.

Set your hardened-off transplants out in their new garden home on a cloudy day to minimize the stress that drying sun and wind add to the shock of transplanting. Have the planting site prepared before bringing the plants out, with the soil adequately moistened. After planting, firm the soil and water in well. Your new plants are off to an excellent start.

CHAPTER 2

MAKING THE MOST OF IT

For gardeners living in USDA hardiness Zones 3, 4, and 5, the issue isn't simply cold temperatures during winter, but late spring and early autumn frosts too. Southern New Hampshire, where I live, can expect a growing season from about May 30 until about September 10. The local rule of thumb is to set plants out just after Memorial Day. The area around Concord, New Hampshire, is Zone 5, but many experienced gardeners plant as though it were Zone 4. Here we often see winter injury to plants rated for Zone 5. Some magnolias, for example, do well, but a year without bloom or a winter of serious damage is not uncommon. Nurserymen frequently assign the plants they sell a hardiness rating, and of course it is sensible to purchase plants with an eye to this, but there is more to hardiness than whether a given plant consistently survived periods of -10°F weather during garden trials. Many things affect the "hardiness" of a plant (see page 4). If it has put on good growth during the rest of the year, it is better equipped to come through a particularly harsh winter in healthy shape.

In this essentially green border, variety is provided by both the type and the hue of the foliage. The dramatic blue tones of the blue oat grass (Helictotrichon sempervirens) *are echoed by the spruce and, back across the greensward, a tremendous thistle.*

Time is in short supply for any gardener, and that seems to go double for gardeners in colder climates. Calculate how long your growing season is likely to be. If you are unsure just how long a growing season to count on, check with your gardening neighbors and your local county extension agent. The "days to maturity" figure many catalogs give for each type of seed is often counted not from the day seed is sown, but rather from the day started plants (typically 1 inch tall) are set out in the garden. You may need to call the seed company to determine whether the information given as "days to maturity" is based on sowing seed directly into the garden or on setting out seedlings. When every day warm enough for growing is precious, you don't want to make an error that costs you a week or longer.

Get acquainted with the climate of your property. Invest in a thermometer that records minimum and maximum temperatures. The more elaborate thermometers may produce graph printouts and run on batteries or electricity. Less elaborate models feature little pins pushed by columns of mercury: A pin marks the coldest and the hottest readings of the day, and once you've had a chance to record those temperatures, you reset the pins for the next day. Noting temperature is an interesting exercise, for it puts you in touch with the rhythm of your garden's world. It will give you one accurate gauge of your garden's microclimate.

GETTING STARTED

Where you site your garden (if you have a choice) will affect your success with many plants. First and foremost, site for best sun. Landscape designer Jessie Woodward, who practices in upstate New York, says morning sun (from sunrise to 3 P.M.) is the most valuable in colder areas, as it warms best and heats longest. Every bit of warmth (except during the dog days of summer) is important, so keep plants out of strong, drying winds. Make use of the shelter provided by buildings, walls, fences, other plants, hills, even ditches (see page 5 for a discussion of windbreaks). Buildings and garden walls of stone or brick hold the day's heat and radiate it at night, warming the area considerably.

A location on a south-facing hillside might gain as much as a couple of weeks in spring and a couple of weeks in autumn. Not only does it enjoy maximum sun exposure, but the colder air slips down the hillside to rest in the valley; at higher elevations, frost comes off the hill. Look around the geography of your property and note where frost pockets may be. If you plant on sloping ground, do so with an eye for "air drainage." The more tender of your plants would probably be less happy near the ground at the bottom of a sloping grade, where cold air collects. Anything growing (or constructed) on a slope, however, blocks the flow of cold air on its way down, creating a cold pocket above the obstruction, a warmer spot below.

When planting seed out in the garden, don't be tempted to sow more deeply than recommended, thinking it will protect the seed better, or keep it warmer. You want the seed to germinate as quickly as possible and the seedlings to have as much time as possible to grow strong quickly. Let them get up into the sunlight and begin making their own food as rapidly as possible. If you plan to sow in cold or very cool, moist soils early in the season, look for seed that has been treated with fungicide. Treated seed is less likely to rot under these conditions. To accommodate seed that likes warm soil, you can prewarm the ground by covering it with plastic mulch at least a week before planting. Black plastic mulch is fine for this, but the recently developed IRT (infrared transferring) green mulch heats the soil more rapidly; for more on the new plastic mulches, see page 27. Warming the soil is highly recommended for heat-lovers such as eggplant and cucumber, among numerous others. It's a boon not only for seeds, but for fussy transplants, too.

SHORTCUTS AND SEASON-EXTENDERS

Make the most of shortcuts available to you. If you can find plants early in the season, go ahead and start with nursery stock — the largest, most vigorous individuals you can find. Otherwise, bringing up your own transplants early ensures you'll have the varieties you desire. Many of the row covers and similar devices (page 7) that protect from cold weather can also provide the warmer environment seedlings require; a row cover enables you to plant earlier and harvest longer.

Greenhouses and Cold Frames

A greenhouse is a luxurious advantage, allowing the gardener to extend the growing season in both directions. While that grand end of the scale isn't an option for many of us, you might want to invest in a modest, prefab "patio" greenhouse with shelves enclosed in translucent plastic, or a similar structure. Win-

Protection for Single Plants

It's possible to approximate greenhouse conditions right in the garden. For individual plants, there are glass cloches or bell jars in various sizes. Some have removable caps for ventilation; those without can be carefully propped open as desired. A homemade cloche can be constructed easily by cutting the bottom from a plastic milk jug. Another commercial gadget called a "greenhouse umbrella" (it looks just like a clear plastic umbrella without a handle) can be set over a collection of pots or plants in the garden. Though the invention called the "Wall-o-Water" won't win any beauty contests, it does a very good job of warming the environment for a single plant. It looks like a teepee of water-filled, clear plastic cylinders, open at the top. Best known for helping tomatoes ripen weeks earlier, it can protect other heat-lovers too.

dow greenhouses offer such an environment in miniature. Of course, the proverbial sunny windowsill has probably brought up more seedlings than all the different sorts of home-gardener greenhouses combined, but early spring light in the North is inclined to feebleness, and can be improved on; see page 20. If you use a sunny windowsill, take care that nighttime temperatures there don't imperil your seedlings.

The most versatile season-extender of all may be the cold frame. This is usually a sort of bottomless box with a sloping clear plastic, fiberglass, or glass lid that can be propped open to several degrees to regulate heat. Woven polyethylene is one of the newest materials that can be used in making a cold frame, for a soft-sided or soft-topped sort of structure. There are lots of types of cold frames from which to choose, whether you buy one or build it yourself. For directions for building a cold frame, refer to *Taylor's Weekend Guide to Backyard Building Projects* (see page 33).

Set the cold frame directly out over the seedbed, or use it as a nursery or staging area for hardening off seedlings. It should be oriented so the sloping lid faces south. For all its simplicity, the cold frame produces mighty results. The temperature inside may be anywhere from 7° to 20°F warmer than outside. The effect of sunlight is concentrated, even on overcast days. Chilling wind can't reach cold-frame residents. Excessive evaporation ceases to be a worry with a cold frame, as does excessive rainfall. Desiccation, rot, and freezing aren't the threats they are "outside."

With a hothouse nursery of even modest dimensions, favorite plants can be helped to reach maturity much earlier in the season.

There are dozens of commercial cold frames on the market, most made with wood or aluminum boxes. Gardeners use what's available, though, and almost any wind-blocking material can be pressed into use. Cold frames for the thriving gardens up at Canterbury Shaker Village (Canterbury, New Hampshire) have long been fashioned of hay bales surrounding a base of rotting (that is, fresh when installed) horse or poultry manure, over which a soil bed is prepared, and the top covered with glass. In "hot beds" like this, the decomposition of the bottom layer generates heat that warms the soil layer for the young plants growing above. It is difficult to know whether a manure hot bed is *too*

New varieties, which may seem so tempting in photographs and the rhapsodic descriptions of gardening friends, may be obtainable only as seed.

hot unless one has the evidence: virtually cooked plants. Electric soil cables, for use in conjunction with a cold frame, are higher-tech alternatives that provide heat that can be regulated.

It's wise to install a thermometer in the cold frame. Plants accustomed to the nearly tropical temperatures of an overindulgent cold frame won't be able to cope as well with the much cooler temperatures to be expected in the dead of winter. Don't let the temperatures in your cold frame go much above 60° to 65°F in autumn and spring. This artificial microclimate can get so hot as to distress or kill the plants inside, so someone must be on hand daily to adjust the venting of, and thus the temperature inside, the cold frame. There are cold frames fitted with automatic venting devices, not an inexpensive feature, but handy and freeing for the gardener. (For hardening off in a cold frame, see page 11.) Cold nights and even a series of cold, overcast days often require that you insulate the cold frame further, with anything from blankets and rugs to commercial home insulation. Don't forget to water plants growing in a cold frame. The warmer the climate inside, the more moisture will evaporate. The plants will require less water in fall and early spring, more in summer when the temperature climbs.

Starting Seed Indoors

You can start seed in pots (clay or plastic), empty yogurt or milk cartons, six-packs, plugs (preformed blocks of peat) or soil blocks formed of potting mixture pressed in a hand-held gadget. Another gizmo forms pots of old newspaper. Plugs, soil blocks, and newspaper pots can be set right into the garden soil at transplant time because the "containers" decompose — easy treatment for transplants made anxious when their roots are disturbed. You can use an open tray or flat to start your seedlings, but then you must very gently separate the seedlings' entangled roots when moving them to larger pots, as soon as their true leaves form. Roots can be cut apart, but it is better if they can be gently teased apart with fingers, pencil, or chopstick. Whatever the container, it must provide for good drainage and allow the growing medium to be at least 3 inches deep. It must be absolutely clean, for disease is easily spread to seedlings, and the usual reason for seedling death is damping off. Though damping off is caused by a number of diseases, all result in the same sad end: the seedling weakens just above the soil line and keels over dead. Seed treated with fungicide is less susceptible to some of the causes of damping off, but there is no substitute for careful preparation of containers and growing medium. Use containers as close to sterile as possible.

Unless garden soil has been sterilized, by heat or chemical means, it should not be used as a growing medium for starting seed. Shepherd Ogden, founder and president of the Cook's Garden in Vermont, recommends a commercially prepared soilless potting mix containing a good amount of peat moss. He advises against packing it down—the tiny emerging plants can put out their roots more easily in a loose medium, one that leaves space for necessary air between soil particles. Moisten the medium thoroughly before planting, and never allow it to dry out. Nor should it ever be actually wet. You can mist seedlings to water them, or set them in a larger tray and water from the bottom. Use water at room temperature. Check your seedlings at least once a day to ensure there is sufficient moisture. Rotate the containers if the plants seem to be growing crooked. Although the ideal temperature for germination of individual seed types varies, many manage at ordinary room temperatures (68° to 72°F). You can probably find slightly cooler or warmer spots around the house for the more particular seeds. A convenient way to provide warmth is with bottom-warming electric heating mats, cables, and tapes, which maintain even heat at the temperature you select. Many experienced cold-climate gardeners feel there's an argument to be made for the bottom heating of seedlings; they report that they are quicker to germinate, and produce more vigorous growth both above and below the soil line.

Emerging seedlings need the strongest light available. A good lighting system is a "cool white" fluorescent bulb or a "grow light" suspended a few inches from the tops of the growing seedlings. If the light source is more than 6 inches from the tops, the young plants will stretch for light, resulting in leggy seedlings. Seedlings will thrive on as much as 16 hours of light per day. Good light and a sufficiently moist growing medium are critical. Once the seedlings have grown a pair of true leaves (not the cotyledon, or seed, leaves), they will appreciate some additional food. Mr. Ogden fertilizes seedlings every third or fourth watering with a dilute combination of fish emulsion and liquid seaweed. Thin seedlings as directed by variety. Crowded seedlings aren't as vigorous and resilient. To avoid disturbing the roots, thin the infant plants using a pair of small scissors to cut off unwanted seedlings at the soil line.

Planting crops as the growing season progresses stretches the harvest period.
Occasionally, it affords such pretty sights as this fall-planted spinach in snow.

A good snowfall prettily mantles structure and plant alike and prods the gardener to consider landscape shapes in their sparer circumstances.

Good Garden Practice

It seems there are always pressing tasks for the gardener. Make the most of the time you have. Prepare your garden beds in autumn, amending the soil as necessary then. If you leave this job until spring, it will be *late* spring before the ground is dry enough to be worked, and you'll lose precious planting and growing time. Let soil amendments work for you over winter, decomposing and enriching your beds while you pore over seed catalogues.

Good garden practice is a must. Obviously, whatever you can do to encourage your plants is all to the good. Fall clean-up is important. Not only is it something you probably won't want to face in spring, when there are so many other pressing and exciting chores, but it is better for your plants if you remove debris such as dead leaves, twigs, branches, and chunks of bark earlier. Insects overwinter happily in garden litter, and disease can be transmitted nicely too. Be vigilant about weeds, especially if you want seedlings to perform. Mulch between vegetable rows to reduce the evaporation of moisture from the soil and discourage weeds. Where there is no mulch, cultivate the soil carefully until your plants have grown large enough to shade out weed seedlings. Treat insect infestations or disease as quickly as you can. The early, judicious use of the appropriate treatment is the safest for your plants, for you and for all the other garden residents. Use nontoxic measures to try to eliminate the problem.

Make the most of the resources available to you. Sufficient praise can't be heaped on the experts at local county extension agencies. There seems no end to their knowledge, patience, and conscientious advice. Some catalogs can be of great help. Johnny's Selected Seeds, for example, discusses individual cold tests, and can be of assistance when you need information to help you make up your mind. In fact, many catalogs welcome questions. Local and national gardening societies offer opportunities to learn about the areas of gardening that interest you most.

During the winter months, once the color of blossom and leaf is gone, assess the structure of your garden. During bitter weather we have the opportunity to examine the garden from indoors and think about the views framed by windows. Are there permanent features of a view you like, yet are able to see only when the landscape is bare of foliage? You can enhance a pleasing aspect and improve a bad view. Evergreens can be very useful for creating screens, structure, and focal points in the winter landscape, but they aren't the only solutions. Observing a stripped-down landscape, you can appreciate pleasing features hidden at other seasons—you can subtract as well as add! Make long winters count. Many shrubs, trees, and ornamental grasses are gorgeous in winter. Try to envision your garden years from now. And while you're planning and plotting, consider some subtle outdoor lighting, for it is a treat to enjoy the drama of the winter garden at night.

CHAPTER 3
THE SHORT-SEASON VEGETABLE GARDEN

There is every good reason to grow vegetables except economy. Take into account the time and labor you've spent on your vegetables and you can see that the yield doesn't entirely offset those "costs," which are real enough. But growing your own vegetables ensures that the food you bring to your table is free of pesticides and herbicides, and vegetables bought at the supermarket can't compete with the flavor of homegrown produce. Finally, growing your own vegetables enables you to indulge yourself with precisely those you want most, whether they be choice strains of snap peas, heirloom beans, exotic-looking little beets, or perfect tomatoes, all of which are available in incredible variety.

CHOOSING A LOCATION

The success of your vegetable garden depends on five factors: location, length of season, soil, good drainage, and fertilizer. Full sun is critical. When choosing a spot for the vegetable garden, site it out of the shade of trees or structures, and well away from thirsty tree roots. If space is very limited, you can always plant

Locating your vegetable garden near your kitchen means that you're more likely to incorporate fresh vegetables in quick meals.

Raised beds ensure excellent drainage and allow you to start some plants earlier, as the soil warms sooner in the spring. Contained gardens also need less maintenance to look well tended.

potatoes and vining crops in a fallow mulch pile. Plant your perennials (rhubarb, Jerusalem artichokes, and asparagus) in a permanent location, and plan to rotate your annual crops. Locate your tall growers on the north side of the garden.

SELECTING VARIETIES

Before succumbing to the allure of seed catalog copy, calculate the number of frost-free days you are likely to have for your growing season. If you can dependably look forward to 85 frost-free days, ask yourself whether it makes sense to give in to the attractions of a lima bean variety that requires 92 days to reach maturity when set out in the garden as started plants. Perhaps the greatest challenge for vegetable and fruit breeders is to achieve a plant that is both significantly early *and* vigorous enough. Dr. Brent Loy of the University of New Hampshire explains that early fruit can prove very taxing on a plant that may not have adequate vegetative growth to survive; once the fruit starts enlarging, the vegetative growth shuts down. The problem is to develop an optimal ratio of fruit to foliage, and breeders work year in and year out to improve varieties. Meanwhile, don't make the mistake of planting too early in hopes of getting the longest possible growing season. Some cool-weather crops, such as beets, carrots, parsnips, radishes, turnips, rutabagas, peas, Brussels sprouts, and cabbage, can endure some frost, but other crops resist efforts to be rushed this way.

MULCHING

For these and other cool-weather crops—lettuce, cabbage, broccoli, potatoes, cauliflower, chard, spinach, and turnips—let the soil warm, then mulch around the started plants. This keeps weeds down and conserves moisture. If your summers are cool, don't apply a thick organic mulch around warmth-lovers such as tomatoes, peppers, melons, and grapes, or pumpkins, squash, eggplants and similar plants, until late in the season, because that sort of mulch reduces radiant heat. Instead, use a black plastic, green IRT (infrared transferring), or red plastic mulch to warm the soil.

These new green and red plastic mulches are exciting developments. They warm the soil, and some of them enhance sunlight. The best way to water plants grown with plastic mulch is via drip irrigation laid beneath the plastic. If this isn't an option, moisten the soil *thoroughly* before putting down plastic mulch. Once the plastic is in place, there will be little evaporation, and no weed competition, so additional water won't be necessary for about six weeks after planting. After that, water around the perimeter of the plastic and around the plant stems where they come through it.

Plastic Mulches

Green and red plastic mulches (the green developed by Dr. Brent Loy, the red by Dr. Loy in collaboration of Dr. Otho Wells, both of the University of New Hampshire) have been shown to increase yield by adjusting the quality of light reflected up to the plants. For growth and yield, plants need light in the red and blue spectra. Dr. Wells finds the red plastic works very well for tomatoes, and reasons that it may help peppers and eggplant too; ongoing testing may bear that out. He points out that red plastic doesn't help every crop, though—for cucurbit family members such as squashes, melons, pumpkins, and watermelons, green plastic gets better results. Loy and Wells are not certain why but suspect it may be in part due to the lush foliage canopy that cucurbits push out, which cuts down on reflection.

Give your vegetable plants every advantage in their brief growing season by using good gardening practices. Improve your soil in autumn. Select seed of cultivars that are disease-resistant and rotate crops from one year to the next, to alleviate the problems of soil-borne diseases. At its simplest, crop rotation means planting crops of the same family in a different bed each year. Brassicas, for example, are prone to clubroot (a fungus that likes acid soil), which can lay your crop of broccoli or cabbage low. Although a good sprinkling of wood ashes will help control clubroot, it is better to rotate your crops to avoid perpetuating the fungal problem.

Succession sowing is nice in theory, but a second crop is usually too much to hope for in areas with the shortest growing seasons. A small-scale alternative, and a very useful trick, is to transplant your thinnings, as of lettuce. The tiny plants will look nearly dead at first, but after a week of daily watering, most should be fine and on their way to providing you with a new crop a week or two after your original sowing.

The dates to maturity given on the following pages are counted from the time of direct seeding out in the garden, or from setting out transplants, depending on the vegetable. If you are in doubt about how long it will take your vegetable to mature, refer to the seed packet, or call the seed company.

The Best and Worst Vegetables for a Short Season

Some vegetables aren't unreasonably demanding of time or effort. By growing them yourself, you are assured of flavor that surpasses that of market vegetables and of getting types frequently unavailable commercially. Among the best vegetables for a short season:

- Beets
- Carrots
- Cucumbers
- Eggplants
- Lettuce
- Peas
- Peppers
- Snap beans
- Squash
- Tomatoes

The least rewarding vegetables for a short season:
- Artichoke: requires a long season of hot weather
- Celery: requires fussy care
- Lima bean: takes too long, often mealy
- Brussels sprout: prone to pests and diseases (and often the gardener is the only family member who will eat them)
- Cauliflower: frost-sensitive, prone to pests and diseases
- Onions/shallots and garlic: takes a long time to grow what commercial growers grow well
- Horseradish: good quality commercially available
- Dry beans: takes a long time, good quality commercially available
- Sweet potato: frost-tender and requires a minimum of 90 days

Arugula

■ Arugula

This delightfully peppery green grows well in cooler weather. Mature plants will go to seed quickly after a series of hot days, resulting in leaves too bitter for some gardeners; remove flower stalks as soon as they appear, and harvest young leaves regularly. Sow arugula directly in the garden every three weeks beginning in midspring for a continuous supply of tender young plants. Or harvest leaves regularly from a summer or *early* autumn crop. Arugula matures in about 40 days.

■ Asparagus

Plant one-year roots ("crowns") as soon as the soil is dry enough to work in midspring. The following spring will yield a modest harvest, and every spring after that you can look forward to plenty of tender spears. A planting trench six to eight inches deep (gradually filled in over the first summer; follow the instructions that accompany the crowns) should keep these perennials safe from frost heaves; keep the plants well mulched from that first midsummer onward. (To enjoy asparagus at its earliest every spring, you may temporarily remove the mulch after your last hard frost, so the bed warms more quickly; still, this seems a lot of work for a small advantage, because the mulch should be replaced as the season continues.) 'Mary Washington UC 72' is earlier, larger and more uniform than that old reliable, 'Mary Washington'.

■ Beans (Leguminosae)

All bean plants are frost-tender. They take about eight days to come up, so you mustn't direct-sow more than a week before your last frost. The problem is always this: When *will* your last frost occur? If you plant too soon, the seed may rot in cold, wet soil, and young plants may be damaged by frost. Dwarf types are hardier and produce earlier. You can plant in hills for warmth, six seeds to a hill, then thin to three or four plants per hill. Some gardeners advocate soaking bean seed overnight to soften the seed coat and speed germination; but if the seed has been treated with fungicide, soaking will most likely wash it off, and planted in cold, wet soil, the unprotected seed may not germinate. Soil innoculant usually increases yields when beans are grown in a plot for the first time.

Fresh beans. These include lima, butter, snap, flat, and filet. You can choose bush or pole types; the bush types mature earlier. Green or yellow (wax) snap beans are ready to harvest soonest of all, and for some gardeners that may be reason enough to plant varieties of these exclusively. Plant every two to three weeks, allowing enough time for the final crop to mature before autumn frosts. Early varieties of "stringless" bush snap green beans include 'Earliserve' (45 days), 'Provider' (50 days), 'Bountiful' (49 days), 'Burpee's Tenderpod' (50 days), 'Slankette' (53 days), 'Improved Tendergreen' (53 days), 'Purple Pod' (51 days), and 'Burpee's Stringless' (52 days). Flat Italian-style beans include 'Roma II' and 'Early Bush Italian', both 50 days. Early bush wax beans include 'Improved Golden Wax' (51 days), 'Brittle Wax' (52 days), and 'Cherokee Wax' (53 days). Of filet beans, 'Triumph de Farcy' requires 48 days, and 'French Filet' and 'La France', 56 days. The purple bush snap bean 'Royal Burgundy' (51 days) is good for cooler soils.

Shell, Broad, and Drying Beans

If you want to gamble on a longer season, choose early varieties of such beans as lima, kidney, mung, broad, and soybeans. To grow that old-fashioned favorite, the broad bean (*Vicia faba*, aka fava, horse, windsor, and tick bean), start indoors and set out in a cold frame about four weeks before the last expected frost, as an alternative to sowing directly at the same time as peas. Don't delay planting, as cool weather is best for growth. Note that the shells, or pods, are frost-tender. Depending on variety, harvest will be in 65 to 90 days. Fresh shell beans tend to require 70 to 80 days; dry beans, 88 to 104, with some of the "novelty" beans, such as adzuki (*Vigna angularis*), requiring 118 days.

Bush snap bean 'Royal Burgundy'

Beet 'Chioggia Striped Beet'

■ Beet

Plant two to three weeks before the expected last spring frost. (The seed will germinate at temperatures as cool as 45°F.) Do not neglect to thin your beets; each "seed" is in fact a little seed pod, so lots of plants will probably come up; the first thinnings, about three inches high, are a delicacy in early-season salads, and a second thinning yields exquisite baby beets. Given insufficient water or left too long in the soil, beets become woody. 'Early Wonder' (57 days) is earlier than some, but if you are very eager, start plants indoors or in a cold frame five to six weeks before you plan to set them outdoors. 'Scarlet Supreme' needs 48 to 50 days, 'Chicago Red', 49 days. 'Chioggia Striped Beet' (50 days) displays bull's-eye rings when sliced. 'Golden Beet' and 'Kleine Bol' both mature in 50 days, and 'Ruby Queen' and 'Sangria', 52 days.

■ Broccoli

Harvest the principal heads, and secondary heads or side shoots will develop in time to enjoy before the end of even a short season. Set out plants right after your last frost or sow directly as early as two weeks before that. Varieties bred for heat- and cold-stress tolerance make the most of a short season. 'Bonanza Hybrid' and 'Green Goliath' mature in 55 days. 'Green Valiant', 59 days, is particularly frost-tolerant. 'Packman F1 Hybrid' (60 days) is good for spring or fall harvest. 'Superblend' also begins harvest at 60 days. 'Marathon', which matures later than most, can be harvested into autumn. Also consider broccoli raab, a broccoli relative with numerous varieties that mature considerably earlier than regular broccoli (about 60 days). Its tolerance for light frost, commercial scarcity, and wonderful flavor also recommend it for home gardening.

■ Cabbage

Varieties identified as "midseason" and "storage" are best bets for the short grow-ing season. 'Roulette', 105 days, is a frost-hardy salad cabbage. Among the ear-liest are 'Fast Ball' (45 days), 'Salad Delight' (50 days) and 'Early Jersey Wakefield YR' (60 days). 'Ruby Ball' is a 72-day red. 'Golden Acre' (64 days) produces a handsome, round head, and 'Dynamo Baby' (70 days) produces baby heads. Chi-nese and Napa cabbages are quicker to mature, and offer a nice change of pace. Start the seed in larger-than-usual plugs; the little plants tend to suffer a check in growth when moved. 'Orient Express' is ready in 43 days. Harvest heads on the small side; they are ready sooner, and a little cabbage can go a long way. Try also 'Copenhagen Market' (68 days); and 'Nagoda' (50 days), 'Jade Pagoda' (68 days) and 'Michihili' (75 days) are Chinese cabbages.

■ Carrot

Choose shorter varieties if you have heavy or very stony soil, or if you want quick maturation. Sow outdoors as soon as the soil can be worked. Thin twice (as for beets); the second thinning yields juicy, pencil-thin roots. Some improved early varieties are sweet even when harvested at the height of summer's heat: 'Cru-sader' is an American, early-bearing hybrid, 65 days, and 'Primo Hybrid' is 65 also. 'Chantenay Royal' matures in 68 days, 'Bolero Hybrid Nantes' and the curi-ous yellow 'Sweet Sunshine' in 72 days.

■ Chard

More cold- and heat-resistant than spinach and with a juicier crunch, chard is a happy addition to the cold-climate garden, continuing to produce until the soil begins to freeze. Some chards will bolt if the young plants are exposed to frost, so direct-sow or set out transplants accordingly. It is important to thin your crop; you can use your thinnings for greens. 'Lucullus' (50 days) and 'Ford-hook Giant' (55 days) are good producers. 'Argentata', an Italian heirloom, and 'Bright Lights', in fireworks colors, both take 55 days. Narrow-leafed chard (*B.v.* ssp. *chicla*) tolerates frost better than Swiss chard, and when grown in the win-ter cold frame can be harvested by cutting and will grow again; try 'Erbette Leaf'.

■ Corn, Sweet

Everyone makes the point that growing corn takes up a lot of room. Still, if you must have it — and if you are willing to gamble that the raccoons and corn borers will allow you to keep some ears for yourself — then set aside a block of modest size for planting. Remember that wind carries pollen from the male to the female plants, so for a good yield of kernels, don't plant in rows, but in squares, to increase the chances of pollination.

Corn is emphatically a warm-season crop, and the seed is inclined to rot in cold, wet soil; for this reason, many varieties of commercially offered corn seed are treated with fungicide. Corn seed will not germinate in soil colder than 55°F, so be patient until conditions are right for sowing. Vegetables need lots of good sun exposure, and this is doubly true of corn. Plant on a site in full sun only (with some thought as to the shade the growing corn plants will cast), in warm soil. Hybrids have been selected for greater tolerance to frost. Seed catalogs offer appealing choices, so pick your way through the descriptions with an eye for early-ripening varieties, and for those developed for "cool-soil vigor."

Sweet Corn for a Short Season

Hybrid corn:
'Early Sunglow' (63 days)
'Quickie' (65 days)
'Seneca Horizon' (65 days)
'Seneca Star' (66 days)
'Trinity' (68 days)

Early, open-pollinated corn:
'Ashworth' (69 days)
'Double Standard' (73 days)

'Earlivee' — a reliable 65-day variety (the seed is not always treated)

Hill Planting

Many northern gardeners swear by planting corn in hills rather than rows. The venerable Samuel Ogden recommends the following technique in *The New England Vegetable Garden* (The Countryman Press, Woodstock, Vermont, 1957), and it is hard to improve on it: A block or grid of holes is dug, each 30 inches apart. To form each hill, a shovelful of soil is set aside and the hole filled by the same quantity of compost. This is tamped down and covered with half a shovelful of the removed soil. Four or five kernels are planted per hill, and each hill then receives the remaining half-shovelful of soil, to cover the corn seed. Thin the plants, so strong-growing seedlings compete for sunlight as little as possible. Hill up around the plants when they are a few inches tall. Cultivate among the young plants as needed to control weeds, then apply mulch when they reach 10 or 12 inches tall, to discourage weeds and keep moisture in the soil. Don't mulch much earlier, or the soil will take longer to warm.

Cucumber 'Tamra Hybrid'

■ Cress

Also known as broadleaf cress. Because this green grows so rapidly, it makes sense to harvest the plants directly from the flat in which the seeds were sown. Sprouts are often ready to harvest in less than two weeks, mature greens in 45 days. Plant successively throughout the season, bringing the flat into a protected area at night when end-of-season frosts are expected. Upland cress, 50 days, is slow to bolt.

■ Cucumber

Seed can be sown directly in the garden just about the time of the last spring frost, but be vigilant: A light frost will put an end to your cucumbers, whether they are seedlings or mature plants. The soil must warm to at least 50°F for any of the seed to germinate; the ideal soil temperature is 85°F. Transplants are a better bet. Sow in pots or larger-than-usual plugs; that way your transplants thrive as soon as they're set out in the garden. Plant in a sunny spot sheltered from wind, for cucumbers thrive in hot conditions, and you want to give them all the heat your situation can muster. Such heat-trapping devices as row covers and cloches will encourage the young plants, but be sure to remove them when the plants are well established if you grow varieties that need pollination. Some gardeners start their plants in a cold frame, planting some out after all danger of frost and leaving some in the cold frame for an accelerated harvest of large fruit. Cucumbers are so heat-loving that you may do well to omit a thick layer of organic mulch around the plants, in order to let them benefit from the radiant heat from the ground (just don't forget to weed); plastic mulches, instead, give warmest results. 'Spacemaster Bush Cuke' (60 days) grows on a compact vine. 'Sweet Burpless' and 'Early Pride Hybrid' (both 55 days) and 'Slicemaster Hybrid' (58 days) are reliably early. 'Tamra' (59 days) is a Middle Eastern variety developed for eating out of hand. 'Northern Pickling' (48 days) is an extra-early, high-yield pickling cuke. For an early "burpless" type, try 'Early Perfection' (62 days) or 'Orient Express' (64 days).

■ Eggplant

Take the trouble to select a location protected from chilling wind, and protect your plants from cold. Choose varieties quick to mature. Start seed indoors about 10 weeks before the last expected frost, or buy plants, and do not set transplants out in the garden until nights are reliably 45°F. Because eggplant seed is demanding (two months of indoor care with soil temperatures of 80° to 90°F, with plenty of moisture), many cold-climate gardeners purchase started plants. Days of 70°F or a little warmer encourage the best growth, and cloches and their kin can be of help here; cool weather can check growth. As with cucumbers and melons, go easy on organic mulch, which keeps the ground from emitting radiant heat, and consider plastic mulch in its place. 'Orient Express' (58 days) is an especially early, elegant, elongated type bred to set fruit in cool weather. 'Little Fingers' (60 days) is a very early "baby" Oriental type, and 'Purple Rain' is a 66-day new hybrid. Eggplant from plants killed by frost will not continue to ripen indoors, so protect plants adequately.

Eggplant 'Orient Express'

■ Endive/Frisee, Escarole

Not so tender as lettuce and apt to bolt in hot weather. Sow in early June for a first crop, early July for an autumn (pre- or post-light-frost) harvest. Plants grown in the protection of a cold frame are often sweeter. 'Tres Fine Endive' matures in 60 days, as do 'Cultivated French Purslane' and 'Salad King'. 'Da Taglio', a frisee, can be started in the heat of summer's end for winter salad from the cold frame. 'Broad-leaved Batavian' produces in 85 days. Radicchio can be sown directly after the last spring frost, or at midsummer if you can chance a late harvest. Look for early-maturing types such as 'Rossana' (about three months). 'Giulio' matures in 80 days and is best started early for planting out just after the frost-free date. 'Firebird', a brand-new introduction, is said to be similar but a more reliable producer.

■ Fennel/Anise

Sweet fennel is the type grown as a vegetable; wild fennel is more often grown as an herb. As fennel requires a long growing season, many find it best to start seed indoors or buy started plants, even though it can be direct-sown outdoors after danger of heavy frost. It is perennial to Zone 5. Cool weather agrees with it; it is apt to bolt in hot weather. Harvest the bulbs before the plants bloom. Fennel might be considered an easily grown alternative to celery, but that sentiment doesn't do justice to its fresh, distinctive flavor. The leaves make a contribution as a fresh herb. 'Romy Fennel', 89 days, is an early heirloom variety.

■ Greens (various; see also Arugula, Cress, Endive, Lettuce)

Claytonia, aka miner's lettuce, is a tasty salad green, best grown in cool weather when days grow shorter; it stands up to mild frost and can grow in greenhouses and cold frames all winter. 'Vit' (50 days) produces happily in early autumn. 'Minutina' (50 days) is one of the most cold-hardy. Corn salad (mache), which will overwinter to 5°F with protection, is planted in late summer, or early fall and early spring. 'Gayla' mache takes 70 to 80 days. 'Mei Qing Choi' pak choi and tat-soi take 45 days. Mustard greens varieties include 'Osaka Purple' (40 days) and 'Green Wave' (45 days).

■ Jerusalem Artichoke

Also known as the sunchoke. Plant this cold-climate native where the tall (often to eight feet) foliage won't block sunlight from neighboring sun lovers. Select a more or less permanent location, as the weedy plants persist for many years. There is no rush to harvest; dig the tubers into late autumn as you need them.

Plant seed pieces (pieces with eyes, cut from tubers) as early as the spring soil is workable. Some northern gardeners report success with sowing seed over virtually frozen ground in autumn, with growth beginning as soon as the soil starts to warm.

■ Kale

Think of kale as a very frost-tolerant green. Of course you wouldn't want to eat the mature leaves raw, but it is very festive to bring something this *leafy* in from the garden so late in the year (many seed catalogs point out that kale can be harvested even in the snow). Sow seed directly about two weeks before the last expected spring frost, with a second sowing in late summer, and thin as directed by variety. Cull baby leaves from selected types to enjoy halfway through the season. Try 'Winterbor (F1)', 28 days to harvest for baby leaves, 60 days mature. 'Red Russian' is ready in 48 days, and 'Dwarf Green Curled Scotch' in 55 days.

■ Kohlrabi

Another cool-weather lover, this vegetable is tailor-made for cold climates. Like the beet, kohlrabi is most tender when harvested young and when raised in soil sufficiently moist to ensure even, rapid growth. Sow twice, in early spring and late summer. 'Kolibri Purple Kohlrabi' and 'Winner (F1)' can be harvested in 45 days, and at 38 days, 'Eder (F1)' is earliest of all.

■ Leek

Even early leek varieties require 80 to 90 days to grow from seed to maturity, so most cold-climate gardeners start their seed indoors in late winter or early spring, or buy transplants. Plant out when as thick as a pencil and water well all season. Established leeks will tolerate some frost, and some varieties have been bred for late fall and even winter harvest (harvest before the ground freezes, though). 'St. Victor' is one such variety, and 'Laura', at 115 days, is extra-hardy for late fall and overwinter harvest. 'Dawn Giant' matures at 98 days.

■ Lettuce

Your lettuce plants will grow most happily with moist soil and during cooler days; hot weather can provoke them to bolt. Head lettuce is more temperamental than leaf lettuce. Most head lettuce requires about three months from seed,

Lettuce 'Buttercrunch'

while leaf lettuce will make do with two. Give your transplants the right start by hardening them off, and they will likely survive a touch of early frost; not so an unprotected maturing head, which will wilt into a sorry mush.

■ Melon

Cold weather can result in chilling injury, and frost is frequently fatal. Dr. Brent Loy of the University of New Hampshire strongly recommends the head start of transplants over direct sowing. He prefers using pots or larger-than-usual plugs for starting plants; then when they're set outdoors (when the soil has warmed to 65°F), they won't be disturbed and suffer a check in growth. Start seed indoors about five weeks before your frost-free date. If you must sow outdoors, sow in hills or a raised bed for the advantage of warmth. Plastic mulch warms the soil and reflects heat back up to the plants; you can simply push seed into the soil through holes punched in the plastic. Melon seed germinates best at soil tempera-

Head Lettuce

Raising head lettuce is an opportunity to exercise your thinning skills, and to use those row covers early and late in the season. Don't be too concerned about warming the soil for sowing; lettuce seed will germinate at soil temperatures as low as 40°F. Start head lettuce seed indoors about six weeks before setting the plants out, or sow out in the garden about two weeks before your frost-free date. Select early-maturing varieties. Types may be crisp-head, cos (Romaine), or butterhead (Bibb). 'Romance' is a 50-day white cos type. 'Winter Density' (54 days) is a Bibb-Romaine, frost-tolerant type that can be grown spring, summer, or fall. 'Bibb' requires 54 days, 'Iceberg', 65 days.

Leaf Lettuce

Start leaf lettuce seed indoors about six weeks before your frost-free date, and set the transplants out in the garden about a month after that. Popular varieties include 'Oakleaf' (40 days), 'Red Sails' (45 days), 'Salad Bowl' (45 days), 'Early Curled Simpson' (45 days) and 'Simpson Elite' (48 days). 'Buttercrunch' is a favorite to start from transplants, 75 days.

tures between 80° and 90°F. Some gardeners warm the soil with a Wall-o-Water a week before planting. Melons appreciate a topdressing of well-rotted manure. As with squash, late-forming fruit should be pinched off, sacrificed to give melons already well on their way the greatest benefit of the time and energy available to the plant in the waning days of the season. Look for early-maturing types (some are tolerant of cool weather).

Cantaloupe: 'Sweet Granite' (70 days), 'Earligold (F1)' (72 days; the earliest large-size cantaloupe) and 'Earliqueen (F1)' (74 days) are derived from cool-weather-tolerant stock developed at the University of New Hampshire. Dr. Loy's 'Earliqueen' has a little more vine in relation to fruit, so it's a strong grower. Dr. Loy also pioneered the honeydew-type 'Passport (F1)' (73 days) and "butterscotch"-type 'Sweetie No. 6 (F1)' (75 days). 'Fastbreak' (65 days) is another early cantaloupe whose flavor may be enhanced by refrigeration. 'Creme de la Creme' is a 75-day hybrid. Some advocate growing the plants with the protection of row covers, plastic tents, hot caps, Wall-o-Water, etc.; this means you may need to hand-pollinate your plants.

Watermelon: The top four inches of soil must be at least 60°F for good germination. Transplants and plastic mulch are recommended. 'Fordhook Hybrid' is ready in 74 days. 'Tiger Baby Icebox' requires 75 days, 'Sugar Baby' 79 days.

■ New Zealand Spinach

The proclivity of spinach to bolt in hot weather is dismaying, so many gardeners turn to New Zealand spinach to avoid this. The good news is that this green adores hot weather; the tradeoff is that it isn't frost-hardy. Direct-sow around the date of the last spring frost and harvest 50 to 80 days later, depending on variety. Select early-maturing types for shorter seasons.

■ Parsnip

As with other vegetables grown from very fine seed, parsnip should be thinned as soon as the little plants are large enough to pull. The seed takes about three weeks to germinate, and the plants require about three months after that. Direct-sow as soon as the soil is ready; soil temperatures as cool as 38°F are not too cold for germination. Dig your parsnips any time in late autumn, winter (if you can find them!), or spring, before the soil warms. The roots can remain in the soil over winter, during which time more of the stored starch will turn to sugar, producing a sweeter parsnip; put down a straw mulch before the ground freezes. 'Harris Early Model' is early: 100 days.

■ Pea

Another cool-weather vegetable. This is traditionally the first crop to be sown outdoors; if soil temperatures climb above 60°F, seed is reluctant to germinate. It has been noted that the smooth-seeded types mature earlier (they are more forgiving of cool weather), but taste less sweet than the wrinkled types. There are many kinds from which to choose, including those with edible pods, shelling peas, which are enjoyed fresh, and other yellow or green peas dried for use in soups and the like. Culture is similar for all. Mulch as soon as your seedlings are growing strong, to discourage weeds and conserve soil moisture. Early green pea varieties include 'World's Record' (57 days), 'Knight' (57 days), and 'Sugar Ann' (52 days). 'Laxton's Progress' is one of the earliest large-podded varieties (64 days). Of edible-pod peas, 'Snowbird' is a very early snow pea, 58 days. 'Norli' and 'Oregon Giant' are 60-day snow peas, and 'Edible Pod' is a 65-day variety.

■ Pepper, Sweet

When it comes to growing members of the family Solanaceae in cold climates, it is commonly acknowledged that peppers are easier to grow than eggplant, though not so easy as tomatoes. Many cold-climate gardeners grow peppers from started plants, for they require about three months; early-maturing varieties are your surest bet, although the fruits tend to be smaller, with thinner walls. If the only way to obtain the variety you desire is by seed, you will have to start your plants indoors (or in a hotbed or cold frame) 8 to 10 weeks before setting them outdoors. Germination is best at soil temperatures about 85°F. Peppers thrive in full sun, preferably in a location protected from chilling wind. Don't use thick organic mulch (plastic's the way to go); the soil needs to be good and warm, and the plants appreciate the radiant heat. Cool nighttime temperatures (50°F) can substantially check growth and fruit set. 'Cadice' is an extra-early (55 days) French hybrid. 'Hungarian Sweet Banana' is ripe in 52 days. 'Ace (F1)' produces green fruit in 50 days, red in 70, and is resistant to blossom drop. 'Yankee Bell' produces green in 60 days, red in 80. For purple-pepper lovers, there is the "chocolate" type; try 'Sweet Chocolate', 58 days green, 78 days brown ripe.

For hot (chili or "ethnic") peppers, see chapter 4, Culinary Herbs.

■ Potato

If you are not put off by the numerous problems that afflict potato crops (among them bacterial and fungal rots, wireworms, grubs, tuberworms, and so on), and long for varieties not found at local markets, then it may make sense to plant this starchy staple. If space is tight, potatoes can be planted right in a fallow mulch pile rather than with the rest of your garden. Early and midseason types are preferable. You can "rob" your plants' hills to harvest some new potatoes, depending on variety. Potato plants like cool nights, but are damaged by frost. (Growth killed by frost may not signal the end of a planting, though, for a plant may send up new growth come spring.) Plant three to four weeks before the last spring frost. Mulch with plastic or organic mulch. 'Early Baby Epicure' (65 days) is very frost-tolerant.

■ Pumpkin — See page 44.

■ Radish

Ready for harvest just three weeks after sowing, the radish has been relegated by some to the status of row marker for other crops that take considerably longer to come up. Though radishes are quick to grow, it is best for northern garden- ers to select early-maturing types; radishes prefer short days, and many varieties may bolt if grown during longer summer days up North. Radish seed germi- nates happily at soil temperatures between 45° and 70°F. The plants thrive in cool weather, so midsummer harvests are not the most successful. Try 'Cherry Belle' (22 days), 'Early Scarlet Globe' (23 days) and 'Roodbol' (24 days). 'Salad Rose', 35 days, is a new Russian variety marketed as excellent for fall crops.

■ Rhubarb

Rhubarb seems unfazed by the grimmest spring weather a cold climate can dish out. Let this hardy perennial get off to a good start: don't harvest the first sea- son, and the year after that, judiciously pull the larger stalks. Let plants get established, and they will reward you with years of harvests — 15 isn't unheard of. The plants benefit from early spring division every four or five years; this actu- ally consists of separating crowns, and very large crowns can be halved and replanted. Make sure every crown has at least one bud. Don't let the crowns dry out when transplanting and dividing.

Some advocate putting rhubarb in a bed of its own; another traditional planting method is to pair it with that other spring perennial, asparagus. Grow in full sun or lightly dappled shade. Good preparation of the bed pays off. Dig a trench some 8 inches deep and a good 3 feet wide. Work in lots of well-rotted manure so the trench is filled with a moist, crumbly, loamy mixture that will drain well. Plant the crowns (rhubarb roots) in early spring, 3 feet apart and a good 2 or 3 inches deep. Remove flower stalks, so the plants put their energy into growth. Organic fertilizer at planting gets the plants going, and a side dressing about halfway through their growth is appreciated. To harvest, pull stalks—don't cut—with a jerk to the side; avoid yanking the crowns. Leave some foliage on each rhubarb plant so it can continue to grow over the summer, but remember that the leaves are toxic. 'Victoria' is a multiple-season variety, and 'Canada Red', 'MacDonald', and 'Valentine' do well in colder climates too.

■ Rutabaga
Some would say hardiness is this vegetable's best attribute. Rutabagas are often confused with turnips, but they require a month longer in the garden. Sow as early in spring as the soil is ready; you will have a fall crop. Rutabaga prefers cool weather, and the roots put on their best growth during the final weeks of the season. Thinning is important. Harvest when roots reach optimum size by variety, and dig any remaining roots before the soil freezes. 'American Purple Top' and 'Burpee's Purple-Top Yellow' each requires 90 days.

■ Spinach
Sow directly in the garden as soon as the soil temperatures reach 60° to 70°F. 'Wolter' loves cool weather and is ready in 37 days. 'Italian Summer' is bolt-resistant and ready in 40 days. 'Bloomsdale Savoy, Long Standing' matures in 45 to 48 days.

■ Squash
Transplants and plastic mulch give you the best results. Row covers will give young plants some protection, as well as discourage insect pests. (If growing open-pollinated types, remove the row covers when the plants produce flowers, so they can be pollinated and produce fruit.) Look for varieties bred for greater

Summer Squash

'Raven' and 'Grey Zucchini' are very early-bearing zucchini (42 days), and 'Milano' is a very productive hybrid that requires the same amount of time. 'Sunburst Yellow Scallop' is an adaptable, early (47 days) crookneck. 'Early Prolific Straightneck' matures in 50 days, as does 'Patty Pan Hybrid'. 'Hasta La Pasta' produces spaghetti squash in 73 days.

Winter Squash

Seed of winter squash germinates best at soil temperatures approaching 70°F, but a good rate of germination is still possible at the brisk temperature of 55°F. Give seedlings and transplants in the garden a boost with cloches or their kin. 'Table Ace Hybrid' produces acorn types in 70 days, 'Early Acorn Hybrid' in 75 days, 'Acorn Bush' acorn in 80 days, 'Table Queen' and 'Cream of the Crop Hybrid' in 85. 'Early Butternut' produces in 83 days.

Pumpkin

'Baby Boo Mini' produces tiny white "ghost" pumpkins in 80 days; 'Munchkin Mini', an orange mini, is ready at the same time. Try 'Racer (F1)', an extra-early (85 days) variety. 'Small Sugar' matures in 100 days.

frost tolerance. As the season draws to a close, several weeks before your first expected frost, pinch female flowers (those with evidence of fruit developing) to no more than four to a plant. You want your squash to put its energy into developing the fruit that may be able to ripen before frost. Protect your vines at night if frost is expected.

■ Tomatillo

There are varieties that mature in from 60 to 100 days, giving gardeners some flexibility. The culture is as for tomatoes, and they appreciate hot growing conditions every bit as much. Some gardeners say they find tomatillos a shade hardier than tomatoes, but the plants will certainly suffer if frosted. The Toma Verde Strain is ready to harvest at 75 days. The paraphernalia that coax tomatoes along faster are excellent for tomatillos.

■ Tomato

Is it practical for you to grow the large-fruiting, late-ripening kinds? You must start them extra early, and grow them indoors before giving them a full summer outdoors to develop their large fruits. Many cold-climate gardeners would give up tomatoes most unwillingly of all, and so it is in growing tomatoes that they gain their greatest experience with heat-conserving technology. Tomatoes are so wildly popular that tomato-growing paraphernalia abounds: cages and towers to support the plants, the redoubtable Wall-o-Water to warm them, special fertilizers, sprays to protect blossom, sprays to stop rot, collars that discourage worms, and more.

Tomato 'Moskovich'

Most varieties require from about 55 to 80 days to mature from seedlings. A new hybrid, 'Fourth of July', is ready in 44 days. The indeterminate (staking) tomato 'Kotlas' (55 days) is cold-tolerant, and indeterminate 'Daniela (F1)' (77 days) has the advantage of a long shelf life (3 weeks), excellent if there is an early, damaging frost. 'Moskovich' (60 days) is an extra-early indeterminate, and 'Dona' requires 65 days. Early determinates (tomatoes that don't require staking) include 'Tiny Tim' (55 days); 'Patio Hybrid', 'Pixie Hybrid', and 'Early Girl Hybrid' (all 52 days); and 'Bush Early Girl' (56 days) and cold-tolerant 'Oregon Spring' (58 days).

For yellow tomatoes, try 'Gold Dust' (61 days) and 'Mt. Gold' (70 days). For a plum tomato, try 'Milano', early-bearing at 63 days. Early-season cherry-types include 'Camp Joy', 'Rose Quartz', and 'Sungold' (65 days), and the so-called patio hybrid 'Tumbler' is very early, 49 days. 'Super Sweet 100 Hybrid' (70 days) is extremely popular.

■ Turnip
Direct-sow anytime from when the soil is first ready for planting until the last expected spring frost. Turnips prefer cooler growing conditions. Varieties will take from about 30 to 55 days. You can harvest baby greens and radish-size turnips. 'Market Express', a Japanese hybrid, is mature at 30 days.

CHAPTER 4
CULINARY HERBS

For better or worse, many herbs are annual. You will have to plant annual herbs every year, but at least you won't need to fret over whether they will survive your winter. As for the perennial herbs, some may require lifting and bringing indoors when the temperature drops, and some will manage with winter protection. As is the case with many other plants, it is the combination of cold *and* wet that kills. Site most herbs in full sun and free-draining soil. An organic mulch will help retain moisture in the soil and keep weeds down.

You can incorporate herbs into flower or vegetable beds, or give them a garden of their own. Some herbs lend themselves to edging walkways, buildings, or borders. Some are delightful ground covers; unless they are particularly drought-tolerant, be sure to site them away from thirsty roots of shrubs and trees. Many herbs can be grown in containers; not only are they ornamental, but they can be moved quite easily this way. Low-growing or trailing herbs are attractive in hanging baskets and shallow pots. If the tenderness of such perennials as lemon verbena, mint, rosemary, and thyme is a concern, you can display them in containers (or sink the pots right into the garden), then bring them indoors when cool weather arrives. Containers — hanging baskets especially — tend to dry out quickly and should be checked daily.

*Harvest culinary herbs early or late in the day,
rather than when the sun is at its peak.*

Ten Herbs Essential to the Cold-Climate Kitchen Garden

- Basil
- Chive
- Marjoram
- Oregano
- Parsley
- Rosemary
- Sage
- Savory
- Tarragon
- Thyme

Ten Hardy Perennial Culinary Herbs

- Chive (Zone 3)
- Lemon balm (Zone 4)
- Lovage (Zone 5)
- Mint (Zone 5)
- Oregano (Zone 5)
- Roman chamomile (Zone 5)
- Sage (Zones 4 to 5)
- Salad burnet (Zones 4 to 5)
- Thyme (Zone 5)
- Winter savory (Zone 4)

Herbs sown directly in the garden won't be ready to harvest until much later in the summer, so start your favorites early indoors, or buy seedlings. The germination rate of many herbs is naturally low, and half an ounce of seed may average 2,500 in number. Consider also that plants may be happiest spaced up to 18 inches apart, and you will see that it is sensible for many gardeners to buy one or a few started plants of the desired herb. Perennial herbs can be started two to three months before your frost-free date, then set out in the garden. Biennial herbs should be started six to eight weeks before the frost-free date and set out at the date; protect them from late-spring frosts. Hardy annual herbs can be started the same time as biennials and can be set out after a month; the seedlings will tolerate some frost. Tender annual herbs will die if frosted, so start them indoors just four to six weeks before the frost-free date and set them out only after that time.

To help your perennial herbs endure winter as best they can, don't harvest from them heavily for about a month before the first autumn frost is expected, for that will encourage the plant to put out tender, new growth.

- Angelica, *Angelica archangelica*

Perennial to Zone 4, often grown as an annual. The handsome, large flower umbels appear the second year. Stratify/prechill seed, and barely cover it. The seed requires some light for germination (which can take a month), and as little as 30 percent of the seed may germinate. Sow in spring or autumn. Locate in partial shade, spacing 1 to 2 feet apart; plants will grow 3 to 5 feet tall.

- Anise hyssop (giant hyssop), *Agastache foeniculum*

Perennial to Zone 4, often grown as an annual. With toothed leaves and purple flower spikes that bloom for a couple of months, the two- to three-foot anise hyssop attracts butterflies and bees to the sunny garden border like a magnet. Some grow the plant for use both fresh and dried for tea, mysteriously described in one seed catalog as "energizing and cooling." The flavor of the leaves and flowers is anisey. The flowers are a pretty addition to cold dishes and baked goods. About three-quarters of seed sown germinates in one to two and a half weeks; direct-sow in spring or autumn, preferably in full sun. The plants grow 2 to 3 feet tall, and should be spaced about a foot apart. It is heat-tolerant with sufficient moisture.

■ Balm, lemon (melissa), *Melissa officinalis*
Often perennial to Zone 4 with protection. The leaves of this two-foot, citrusy individual are a nice surprise in salads and with fruit, and make a delicious tea. You can direct-sow after all danger of frost; germination can take as long as three weeks. Cuttings root easily, but realize lemon balm can be a ferocious spreader; some gardeners grow it in a large container with the bottom cut out. Provide a thick mulch to see it through the winter. It grows well in sun or part shade.

Golden lemon balm (Melissa officinalis *'Aurea'*)

■ Basil, *Ocimum* spp., esp. *basilicum*
Tender annual. Start indoors four or five weeks before transplanting; basil prefers warmer soil, so it is worth waiting until both days and soil are at least 60°F. Rich soil light in texture is the ideal for this sun-loving annual. Provide adequate water for germination and growing on—basil isn't forgiving of drought, and the lightest touch of frost marks the end of the basil-growing season by turning the foliage brown and mushy. There are scores of basils. Some varieties are marketed specifically as "pesto" basils, among them 'Italian Large Leaf', 'Genovese', and 'Mammoth'. Some basils have distinctive aromas, including anise, cinnamon, citrus, clove, and licorice. Foliage may be smooth, serrated, or ruffled, in tones of emerald, lime green, or purple. The flowers, which may be green, pink, or pur-

A riot of basils: 'Purple Ruffles', 'Siam Queen', 'Genovese', licorice, spicy globe, and 'Finissino a Palla'

ple, bring bees to the garden, but should be removed to keep the plants productive. To encourage branching and lusher foliage, pinch back regularly starting when plants are six inches tall. You can't put flowering off forever, though,
so plan on two crops a season, planted three or four weeks apart. 'Purple Ruffles', an especially popular ornamental basil, has large, dark purple, ruffled leaves.
Varieties marketed as "Italian" and "Oriental" are types particular to those culinary traditions; 'Siam Queen' (60 days) is relatively new, with lots of anise.

■ Bay (bay leaf, sweet bay), *Laurus nobilis*
Tender perennial. Place nursery plants or rooted cuttings in pots and set them
outdoors in full sun. Bay is very tender, and should be brought indoors if frost
threatens. It winters over successfully indoors as a handsome house plant.

- **Bergamot (bee balm, Oswego tea, wild bergamot),** *Monarda didyma*

Perennial to Zone 4. The fringed flowers attract bees and hummingbirds. In full sun and moist soil it is an efficient spreader and makes a beautiful ornamental. Lemon bergamot *(M. citriodora)* has deliciously lemony leaves.

- **Borage,** *Borago officinalis*

Tender annual. The cucumber flavor of the tiny blue flowers and tender, young leaves makes a wonderful contribution to salads and a nice accompaniment to fish. The starlike flowers, which hang from the top of plants $1\frac{1}{2}$ to 3 feet tall, are one of the garden's most elegant garnishes. Borage will manage in dappled shade, but prefers sun, and cooler days. Direct-sow after all danger of frost; succession sowing makes removal of ungainly, towering mature plants bearable.

Borage (Borago officinalis)

- **Chamomile (Roman chamomile),** *Chamaemelum nobile;*
  sweet false chamomile (German chamomile), *Matricaria recutita*

Roman chamomile is a perennial hardy to Zone 5. German chamomile is an annual; try 'Bodegold' for flowers two weeks earlier than those of the Roman type. The tiny, daisylike flowers of both chamomiles are used in making tea, scents, and hair rinses. Both types prefer sun and soil on the sandy side.

- **Chervil (French parsley),** *Anthriscus cerefolium*

Annual. Direct-sow after all danger of heavy frost, in partial shade. Transplanting isn't often successful. When happy, the plant grows to 2 feet tall, with finely cut, anise-flavored foliage. Chervil may do well into early autumn, as it tolerates some frost. Improved (unnamed) varieties are more heat- and cold-resistant.

Drying and Freezing Herbs

Herbs are most flavorful or fragrant when freshly picked. Some retain more of their essential oils when frozen, and some when dried. To dry herbs, rinse them clean, thoroughly pat dry, and store protected from dust and humidity. Herbs best for drying include bay, chamomile, chives, dill, fennel, hyssop, lavender, lovage, mints, oregano, rosemary, sage, savory, sweet marjoram, sweet woodruff, tarragon, and thyme.

To freeze herbs, blanch the rinsed foliage in boiling water for one minute, then refresh under cold running water for two minutes to help preserve color. Thoroughly pat dry, then seal in airtight plastic. Herbs that freeze successfully include basil, chervil, chive, coriander, dill, fennel, parsley, sage, salad burnet, and sweet marjoram.

■ Chive, *Allium schoenoprasum*

Perennial to Zone 3. This sun-lover is very ornamental. Clumps of individual, tubular plants grow 1 to 1½ feet tall, with globes of pink, lavender, purple, or white flowers. Garlic chives (*A. tuberosum*) are also very hardy, with an oniony garlic flavor and white flowers. The flowers of both types are edible, and both are easiest to grow from small plants or by dividing clumps.

■ Coriander (Chinese parsley, cilantro), *Coriandrum sativum*

Hardy annual. Increasingly the plant is known as "cilantro," the seeds as "coriander." By pinching off flower heads you can extend your harvest of the spicy, lemony leaves (they look like those of flat-leaf parsley); the ferny, secondary foliage has an acrid flavor. A series of hot (about 75°F) days may provoke the plants to bolt, and once the thick flower spikes come up, harvest of the fresh, flat leaves comes to a rapid conclusion. An especially heat-resistant selection is 'SloBolt'. These annuals enjoy full sun, but some shade may deter bolting. Harvest unripe seed for a lemony, bright flavor that is nice with salads and seafood; the golden brown, ripe seed is indispensable in Indian and Mexican cooking and in baking. As the harvest will last only about a month and a half (and that is if the plants don't bolt), plant successively. Direct-sow the first batch about two weeks before last expected frost, or put out transplants after the last spring frost. Don't be surprised if it reseeds itself.

Dill (Anethum graveolens), *bejewelled umbels early in the morning.*

■ Dill, *Anethum graveolens*

Tender annual. Give this elegant plant a sunny spot in any garden, for its showy flower umbels and 3-foot ferny foliage are lovely. Harvest the delicious foliage and ripe seed. There are dwarf varieties available. Sow directly in the garden in early spring (it dislikes transplanting), or buy nursery stock. 'Bouquet' matures in 68 days.

■ Fennel (Florence fennel, anise, wild fennel), *Foeniculum vulgare*
See Vegetables, page 37.

■ Lemongrass, *Cymbopogon citratus*
Tender perennial. Started plants of this tropical herb will suffer from cold and drying wind, so give them the protection of a heat-retaining wall or corner. Bring indoors for the winter, and keep moist.

■ Lemon verbena, *Aloysia triphylla*
Tender perennial. It makes most sense to buy plants of this slow-grower (annual in the North). Site in full sun in free-draining soil.

■ Lovage, *Levisticum officinale*
Perennial to Zone 5. When growing strongly in full sun and moist, fertile soil, lovage can reach 3 to 4 feet tall. The flavor of the leaves is reminiscent of celery. Propagate by seed or root division in spring or fall.

■ Marjoram (sweet marjoram), *Origanum majorana*
Hardy annual. It's often said that marjoram tastes like oregano, only sweeter. Low-growing in colder climates, it produces pretty, dark little leaves with pungent, savory flavor. It's somewhat tolerant of heat and drought. Set out transplants after the frost-free date.

■ Mint, *Mentha* spp.
Many mints are hardy to Zone 5, and some are considerably hardier. Consider planting this invasive herb in a pot. Sun and good drainage are important, but moist soil is not a problem. Curly mint (*M. aquatica* var. *crispa*, Zone 3), peppermint (*M. × piperita*, Zone 3), and spearmint (*M. spicata*, Zone 4) are must-haves. Apple *(M. suaveolens)*, chocolate, pineapple (*M.s.* 'Variegata'), and many other types are represented in catalogs. Numerous mints don't breed true from seed, so nursery stock or runners are the best bet. Plant in spring and fertilize in late summer.

■ Nasturtium — See page 61.

■ Oregano (Greek oregano), *Origanum* spp.

Perennial to Zone 5 and often Zone 4. Oregano species grow from 6 inches to $1^1/_2$ feet tall in full sun. *O. heracleoticum*, the real Greek oregano (known sometimes as *O. vulgare hirtum*) has the intense flavor we associate with oregano, with a mounding habit and white flowers. A popular new introduction is 'Hopley's Purple Oregano', (*O.* sp.), an ornamental variety with purple stems, purply leaves, and tiny pink blossoms; the flavor is spicy. Ensure good drainage; oreganos are drought-tolerant. Set out hardened seedlings or nursery stock after danger of frost.

■ Parsley, *Petroselinum crispum*

Biennial grown as an annual. Lift and pot up this biennial and bring it indoors to a sunny window for use over winter. Start with new plants each spring for best flavor. The flavor of curly parsley is less pronounced than that of the flat-leaved type, but offers contrast of foliage, or the tidy habit of more dwarf varieties. 'Krausa' curly parsley, a new Dutch introduction, is said to be especially flavorful. Start seed indoors very early, by several months, as it is a fickle germinator; the seedlings are somewhat hardy. Grow in full sun or partial shade. 'Evergreen' matures in 70 days. 'Moss Curled' and 'Frisca Curly' are ready in 75 days, 'Banquet' and 'Italian Dark Green' in 76.

■ Peppers, hot (chili peppers, ethnic peppers), *Capsicum frutescens*

Annual. Start your peppers indoors (March is not too early); they will happily grow outdoors only under the warmest summer conditions, and take their time to mature (most, 68 to 150 days). Champion growers Ann and John Swan start three seeds per cube in Jiffy 7s at about 70°F; they cut all but the strongest seedling off at soil level. Then they pot them up in 4-inch pots filled half with Pro-Mix, half with screened garden soil. They harden the young plants off carefully during a two-week transition. 'Early Jalapeno' (60 to 65 days) is something of a star. Two dependably early varieties are 'Lipstick' (53 days green, 73 days red ripe) and 'Paper Dragon (F1)' (55 days green, 80 red ripe). 'Salsa Delight' is a mildly hot cayenne type, 70 days. From the milder cayenne types and poblanos (called anchos when dried; about 65 days), to chiltepins, Thai dragons, and habaneros (70 to 150 days), hot pepper types abound.

■ Rosemary, *Rosmarinus officinalis*
Perennial to Zone 6. Cold, wet soil is an enemy. In a container, you can grow it on (indoors) for years, and enjoy rosemary's woody stems and dramatic, Mediterranean presence. Leave it in its pot year round; simply bury the pot in the summer garden in full sun. As germination is often disappointing, take plants from friends or nursery stock, or try rooting cuttings or layering.

■ Sage, *Salvia officinalis*
Perennial to Zone 5, sometimes Zone 4. The plants prefer free-draining soil and full sun, and otherwise are slow of growth; in perfect conditions they may reach 2 feet tall. Sage is heat- and drought-tolerant. It can be successfully started indoors six to eight weeks before the frost-free date.

■ Salad burnet, *Poterium sanguisorba, Sanguisorba minor*
Perennial to Zone 5, sometimes Zone 4. This low-growing herb makes a handsome edging, at its best in full sun. Seed can be started indoors if the fussy, taprooted transplants are handled with great care.

■ Savory, *Satureja* spp.
Winter savory *(S. montana)* can make it through Zone 4 winters with some protection, especially from wind; give it good drainage. Buy started plants or propagate by division. Summer savory *(S. hortensis)* is an annual herb. Sometimes known as the "bean" herb, it is a nice addition to lentil, pea, and bean dishes; it is milder in flavor than winter savory. Summer savory grows easily from seed; start indoors six weeks before the last spring frost, and give the seed light to germinate. Winter savory likes lean soil on the sandy side, and summer savory likes it rich.

■ Sorrel (sour grass), *Rumex* spp.
Perennial to Zone 4, sometimes Zone 3. The most frequently grown type is French or garden sorrel, *R. acetosa,* a 2- to 3-foot, large-leaved herb with mouthwateringly tangy flavor. Plant (seed or root division) in full sun or part shade.

■ Sweet cicely, *Myrrhis odorata*

Perennial to Zone 5. Direct-sow in autumn so the seeds' chilling requirement is satisfied. Don't harvest the first year. Sweet cicely prefers light to moderate shade but will manage in full sun. Roots, leaves, and seeds have a sweet flavor reminiscent of licorice.

■ Sweet woodruff, *Asperula odorata*

Perennial to Zone 3. Today this hardy herb is grown more as a spring ornamental than for the preparation of May wine; the whorled foliage and starry white blossoms are lovely. Germination can take six months; place nursery stock (or root divisions from a friend) in part sun in light, moist soil. Work peat moss into the bed.

■ Tarragon, *Artemisia dracunculus*

Tender perennial, hardy to Zone 5. French tarragon is more flavorful than the Russian. Grow from divided plants, tip cuttings, or nursery stock. It will reach as tall as 18 inches in full sun. Once frost has killed some of the foliage, cut the plant to the ground and apply a thick organic mulch.

■ Thyme, *Thymus* spp.

Perennial to Zone 6, many varieties to Zone 5. Established plantings are tolerant of drought. Common or French thyme, *T. vulgaris,* and English broad-leaved thyme are shrubby kitchen staples. In spring, cut old branches back very hard to encourage lots of fresh growth. Creeping thyme, *T. serpyllum,* is another good culinary choice. Most types grow 6 to 12 inches tall in full sun. Some prostrate thymes make pretty carpets. Silver thyme (*T. vulgaris* 'Argenteus') has delicious green and white foliage and a shrubby habit, and may reach 18 inches. Lavender thyme *(T. thracicus)* is named for the appearance of the flowers and the lavender notes in the flavor. Golden lemon thyme *(T. × citriodorus)* is nice for imparting a citrusy edge to sauces and teas. Thymes are usually attractive, perennial ground covers or borders if kept weeded. Some are easily grown from seed, others from rooted cuttings.

CHAPTER 5

ANNUALS, PERENNIALS, AND BULBS

FLOWERING ANNUALS

An annual germinates, matures, and dies all in the span of one brief growing season. Unlike perennials, many bloom all summer long. Flowering annuals are the principal players in some gardens, and in others they fill in color or contrast where needed. Because annuals are relatively inexpensive, it is no great matter if you don't like the way a particular plant turns out—you can start over without many regrets. Gardeners in cold climates should select early-flowering varieties. You can always find a selection of seed packets and young plants at your local nursery, garden center, or even supermarket or hardware store, but for annuals that are less run-of-the-mill, you will probably need to send away for seed from mail-order suppliers.

Most annuals prefer full sun, free-draining soil of good fertility and a pH between 6.0 and 6.5, ample moisture, and some protection from cold wind. If growth seems very slow, apply a commercial fertilizer for flowering plants, or manure tea. Annuals are fairly heavy feeders and need potassium and phosphorus somewhat more than nitrogen, which may favor leaves over flowers. Snip off dead flowers to encourage bloom; if you don't deadhead, your plants will think their job of producing flowers is done.

A mixture of annuals in their glory, among them annual larkspur (Consolida), *mallow* (Lavatera), *and godetia* (Godetia).

Hardy, Half-hardy, and Tender Annuals

A few annuals make good progress in cold climates if sown very early in spring (and some, if sown the previous fall). These are considered "hardy" annuals, and their young plants can endure at least a little frost. "Half-hardy" annuals won't tolerate cold soil—not only will they fail to thrive, but the seeds will stall germination (or just rot), and young plants that aren't fully hardened off suffer from even slight frost. Finally, there are "tender" annuals, which join the party during the hottest days halfway through summer (or even later) and cannot be planted out until after the last frost.

Many young plants are prone to injury or worse from frost, so listen to weather forecasts in late spring, early summer, and early autumn. Not all annuals welcome baking hot summers either; if this describes the July and August weather in your area, you'll want to plant some of the cool weather lovers and more heat-tolerant types. Many forms of protection and season extenders can help in gardening with annuals; see page 15.

There are three ways to bring annuals into your garden: by sowing them out in the garden, starting seed indoors, and purchasing started plants.

Direct Sowing

Sowing annual seed directly where the plants are to grow can be chancy. Many are not quick enough of growth to make a good show before summer's end. There are other drawbacks, too. For one thing, you need to be able to tell a weed from an emerging seedling, because seedlings will suffer if there is much competition from weeds. In addition to weeding, you must thin the seedlings (as recommended by variety) for good results.

To direct-sow annual seed, prepare the soil the preceding autumn. Turn it up thoroughly, and clear it of stones and weeds as much as possible. Work in some compost or well-rotted manure. This is especially important if you wish to grow tender perennials as annuals. Then, just before sowing, go over it lightly with your spade to loosen it, so the emerging plantlets will be able to push their way through it. If the soil looks as though the effects of autumn's amendments fell short of miraculous, work in some compost, but nothing that isn't fully decomposed. Rake the soil surface even and moisten it well before sowing. The seedbed must be kept evenly moist (not wet!) to succeed without bare patches.

In the following listings, the days-to-bloom information is calculated from time of direct sowing.

- Annual baby's breath, *Gypsophila elegans.* Sow in early spring. Bloom at about 45 days. Full sun. Hardy.

- Annual candytuft, *Iberis umbellata.* Sow two to four weeks before frost-free date. Bloom at about 60 days. Full sun or partial shade. Hardy, prefers cooler weather.

- Annual larkspur, *Consolida* spp. Sow in late autumn or early spring. (Transplants very fussy.) Bloom at about 75 days. Full sun or partial shade. Hardy.

- Annual mallow, *Lavatera trimestris.* Sow two weeks before frost-free date. (Transplants very fussy.) Bloom at about 90 days. Full sun. Hardy.

- California poppy, *Eschscholzia californica.* Sow in autumn or early in spring. Bloom may take 60 to 90 days. Full sun. Cool weather lover. Hardy.

California poppy

- Forget-me-not, *Myosotis sylvatica, M. alpestris.* Sow in late summer or early autumn for flowers the following spring. Bloom at about 90 days. Full sun or partial shade. Hardy. Will self-sow.

- Love-in-a-mist (devil-in-a-bush), *Nigella damascena.* Direct-sow in October for bloom the following July. Plants may take 105 days to bloom. Full sun. Hardy.

- Moonflower and morning glory, *Ipomea alba* and *I. purpurea.* Soak seed overnight to speed germination. Sow in late May or start in large plugs a month early; they don't transplant well. Bloom at 90 to 100 days. Full sun. Half-hardy.

- Nasturtium and canary creeper, *Tropaeolum majus* and *T. peregrinum.* Trailing and creeping forms available. Sow fresh seed as soon as soil can be worked. They don't transplant well. Full sun to partial shade. Half hardy. Cool weather lover. Will self-sow. Planted as an herb; buds, flowers, and leaves are delicious. Canary creeper (*T. peregrinum*) is a quick-growing, frost-tender vine. Full sun or partial shade. Half-hardy. Bloom at about 50 days.

Nasturtium

- Portulaca (moss rose), *Portulaca grandiflora.* Sow in early May. Bloom at about 55 days. Full sun. Heat lover. Half-hardy. Will self-sow.

- Shirley poppy (corn poppy), *Papaver rhoeas.* Sow in October or May; they don't transplant well. Bloom at about 80 days. Full sun. Hardy. Will self-sow.

- Sweet alyssum, *Lobularia maritima, Alyssum maritimum.* Sow as early as mid-April. Bloom at about 50 days. Full sun or partial shade. Hardy. Cool weather lover.

- Sweet pea, *Lathyrus odoratus.* Sow as soon as soil can be worked; they don't transplant well. Soak seed to speed germination. Bloom at about 90 days. Full sun or partial shade. Hardy. Cool weather lover.
- Sunflower, *Helianthus annuus.* Sow on your frost-free date. Bloom at about 60 days. Full sun. Heat lover. Tender.

Sunflower (Helianthus annuus)

Starting Annuals Indoors

If you have a convenient spot to serve as a greenhouse, and if you select plants that don't take a very long time to germinate, then this is an excellent way to obtain quantities of your favorite annuals. Use a sterile soilless mixture such as the one described on page 20. Start seed of annuals that are fussy transplants in large plugs, so the roots are disturbed as little as possible when they move into larger pots or into the garden; small plugs may not provide enough of a buffer. If sown in flats, separating the seedlings may inflict more trauma than they can survive. Most seeds germinate best in a particular temperature range, and some need light for germination. All seedlings need light to grow, and if they don't get enough light, they become leggy and weak. See page 19 for information on starting seed indoors.

The following annuals may be started indoors:

- Ageratum (floss flower), *Ageratum houstonianum*. Start two and a half months early; set out after danger of frost. Full sun or partial shade. Half-hardy.
- Blanket flower (Indian blanket), *Gaillardia pulchella*. Start two months early. Set transplants out around last frost date. Full sun. Hardy.
- Brachycome (Swan River daisy), *Brachycome iberidifolia*. Start two months early and set out after danger of frost. Full sun. Half-hardy.
- Calendula (pot marigold), *Calendula officinalis*. Start two months early; set out after danger of frost. Full sun. Hardy. Cool weather lover.
- China aster, *Callistephus chinensis*. Start two months early; set out after danger of frost. Transplants are fussy, so start in large plugs. Full sun. Half-hardy.
- Cleome (spiderflower), *Cleome hassleriana*. Start two months early and set out after danger of frost; or direct-sow in spring. Full sun or partial shade. Hardy. Heat lover.
- Cockscomb, *Celosia argentea*. Start two months early; set out when nighttime temperatures are about 60°F. Full sun or partial shade. Half-hardy. Heat lover.
- Cosmos (Mexican aster), *Cosmos bipinnatus*. Start two months early and set out after danger of frost; or direct-sow as soon as soil can be worked. Full sun. Tender. Heat lover. May self-sow.
- Cup-and-saucer vine, *Cobaea scandens*. Start three months early in large plugs; set out after danger of frost. Full sun. Hardy.
- Cupflower, *Nierembergia hippomanica* var. *violacea*. Start two and a half months early; set out after danger of frost. Full sun to partial shade. Tender, but cool weather preferred.

Blanket flower

Cleome

Annuals That Attract Birds

Some annuals will offer birds a nice treat if allowed to set seed. In and of themselves, these plants probably aren't enough to get birds to notice your garden if they don't already pay the occasional call. But if birds are already visitors to your garden, they may discover that the seed heads of these flowers hold food for them: annual sunflower, China aster, cosmos, forget-me-not, impatiens, marigold, Mexican sunflower, portulaca, and zinnia. As summer draws to a close, you can stop deadheading and let the seed form.

- Four o'clock, *Mirabilis jalapa.* Start six weeks early, in large plugs or pots as transplants are fussy. Soak seed to speed germination. Set out after all danger of frost. Full sun or partial shade. Half-hardy.

- Globe amaranth, *Gomphrena globosa.* Start two months early. Soak seed for a couple of days to speed germination. Set out after all danger of frost. Full sun. Half-hardy.

- Hollyhock, *Alcea rosea.* Start two months early in large plugs and set out after danger of frost, or direct-sow around the frost-free date. Look for strains that flower the first year. Full sun. Hardy biennial.

- Love-lies-bleeding, *Amaranthus caudatus.* Start two and a half months early in large plugs, then move seedlings to 3-inch plastic pots; transplants are fussy. Set out only after frost. Full sun. Half-hardy.

- Phlox, *Phlox drummondii.* Start one to two months early in large plugs; transplants are fussy. Set out after danger of frost, or direct-sow in early May. Full sun. Half-hardy.

- Stock, *Matthiola incana.* Dislikes hot weather, so start two months early, to set out as soon as frost is past. Full sun. Half-hardy.

Buying Started Plants

For the longest summer of annual color, buying plants gives you the best head start. Select sturdy individuals that appear to be growing strongly, and if they are without bloom, all the better — they will settle in and grow on more readily if not yet in flower. If they are outside at the garden center, you can probably plant them right out.

- Balsam, *Impatiens balsamina*. Tender. Partial shade.
- Begonia, wax, *Begonia × semperflorens*. Tender. Prefers some shade.
- Black-eyed Susan vine, *Thunbergia alata*. Tender. Full sun to partial shade.
- Cornflower (bachelor's button), *Centaurea cyanus*. Hardy. Full sun. Cool weather lover.
- Hyacinth bean, *Dolichos lablab*. Tender perennial. Full sun. Warm weather lover.
- Impatiens (busy Lizzie), *Impatiens walleriana*. Tender. Prefers partial shade.

Impatiens

- Lobelia, *Lobelia erinus*. Half-hardy. Full sun or partial shade. Cool weather lover.
- Madagascar periwinkle (annual vinca), *Catharanthus rosea, Vinca rosea*. Tender. Full sun or partial shade. Warm weather lover.
- Marigold, *Tagetes* spp. Half-hardy. Full sun.
- Mexican sunflower, *Tithonia rotundifolia*. Half-hardy. Full sun. Hot weather lover.
- Nicotiana (flowering tobacco), *Nicotiana alata, N. sylvestris*. Half-hardy. Full sun or partial shade.
- Painted tongue, *Salpiglossis sinuata*. Half-hardy. Full sun or partial shade.

Nicotiana

- Pansy (tufted pansy), *Viola cornuta*; pansy, *V. × wittrockiana*; Johnny-jump-up, *V. tricolor,*. Hardy. Full sun or partial shade.
- Petunia, *Petunia × hybrida*. Half-hardy. Full sun or partial shade.
- Pincushion flower (sweet scabious), *Scabiosa atropurpurea*. Half-hardy. Full sun.
- Salvia, red, *Salvia splendens*. Half-hardy. Full sun or partial shade.
- Snapdragon, *Antirrhinum majus*. Half-hardy. Full sun or partial shade. Cool weather lover.
- Verbena, *Verbena × hybrida*. Full sun. Half-hardy.
- Wishbone flower, *Torenia fournieri*. Tender. Partial to full shade. Cool weather lover.
- Zinnia, *Zinnia* spp. Half-hardy. Full sun. Hot weather lover.

PERENNIALS AND BIENNIALS

Although perennials die back to the ground every winter, they will reappear year after year. Many of them increase in size, and can be divided and planted elsewhere in your garden, or shared with friends. Of the vast selection of com-

Lobelia, or cardinal flower (Lobelia cardinalis)

mercially available perennials, many are quite hardy. A listing of some readily obtained plants follows. With a mixture of spring-, summer-, and fall-blooming perennials, you can enjoy continuous color in your garden. Look for long-blooming plants; they'll make summer seem all the longer. Some perennials languish in hot, dry summers; if that describes your summer weather, select types more forgiving of drought. Plant perennials where they will thrive, whether in full sun, part shade, or full shade.

In cold climates, spring is the preferable planting time, for although the soil will be on the cold side, the new plant will have the best chance to establish itself before winter's onset. Peonies and some iris, though, fare better when planted in fall. Prepare your perennial bed well. Make sure the soil is loose, and amend it as necessary. If rain has been sparse, supplement with the garden hose throughout the growing season and into autumn. Mulch well.

Perennials hardy to Zone 2
- Amethyst sea holly, *Eryngium*
- Blanket flower, *Gaillardia*
- Cardinal flower, *Lobelia*
- Common bleeding-heart, *Dicentra*
- Daylily, *Hemerocallis,* Zones 2 to 4, depending on variety

Daylily

Perennial Vines

"Vertical gardening" with perennial vines adds immensely to the landscape. Hardy perennial vines include:
- Actinidia (*Actinidia,* Zone 4)
- Akebia (*Akebia,* Zone 4)
- American bittersweet (*Celastrus,* Zone 3)
- clematis (*Clematis,* Zones 3 to 4)
- Dutchman's pipe (*Aristolochia,* Zone 4)
- Fleece vine (*Polygonum,* Zone 4)
- Honeysuckle (*Lonicera,* Zone 5)
- Hops (*Humulus,* Zone 3)
- Hydrangea (*Hydrangea,* Zone 4)
- Ivy (*Hedera,* Zone 4)
- Porcelain vine (*Ampelopsis,* Zone 4)
- Trumpet vine (*Campsis,* Zone 4)
- Virginia creeper, Boston ivy (*Parthenocissus,* Zones 3 to 4)
- Wisteria (*Wisteria,* Zones 3 to 4)

False dragonhead (Physostegia virginiana)

- False dragonhead, *Physostegia*
- Snow-in-summer, *Cerastium*

Perennials hardy to Zone 3

All plants hardy to Zone 2, plus:

- Baby's breath, *Gypsophila*
- Balloon flower, *Platycodon*
- Bergenia, *Bergenia*
- Bloody cranesbill and bigroot geranium, *Geranium*
- Bugbane, *Cimicifuga*
- Catmint, *Nepeta*
- Columbine, *Aquilegia*
- Coneflower, *Rudbeckia*
- Coralbells, *Heuchera*
- Cornflower, *Centaurea*
- Deadnettle, *Lamium*
- False sunflower, heliopsis, *Heliopsis*
- Fringed bleeding-heart, *Dicentra eximia*
- Gas plant, *Dictamnus*
- Gayfeather, *Liatris*
- Globe thistle, *Echinops*
- Goatsbeard, *Aruncus*
- Heartleaf brunnera, *Brunnera*
- Hellebore, *Helleborus,* depending on variety
- Hosta, plantain lily, *Hosta*
- Iris, *Iris,* depending on variety
- Lady's mantle, *Alchemilla,* depending on variety
- Lungwort, *Pulmonaria*
- Lupine, *Lupinus,* depending on variety
- Mallow, *Malva*
- Meadowsweet and queen-of-the-prairie, *Filipendula*
- Monkshood, *Aconitum*

Coneflower

Monkshood

Oriental poppy (Papaver orientale)

- Oriental poppy, *Papaver*
- Painted daisy, *Chrysanthemum*
- Pearly everlasting, *Anaphalis*
- Phlox, *Phlox*
- Pincushion flower, *Scabiosa*
- Pinks, sweet William, *Dianthus*
- Purple coneflower, *Echinacea*
- Salvia, *Salvia,* depending on variety
- Sea lavender, *Limonium*
- Silvermound, *Artemesia*
- Sneezeweed, *Helenium*
- Stonecrop, *Sedum*
- Turtlehead, *Chelone*
- Wild indigo, *Baptisia*
- Yarrow, *Achillea*

Purple coneflower

Yarrow

Perennial Ground Covers

Hardy perennial ground covers can be the solution plants for problem areas such as steep banks, and they are beautiful underplantings. They are attractive alternatives to lawn and excellent for erosion control. Hardy ground covers include:

- Bugle weed (*Ajuga*, Zones 3 to 4)
- Candytuft (*Iberis*, Zone 4)
- Cinquefoil (*Potentilla*, Zone 3)
- Cotoneaster (*Cotoneaster*, Zone 4)
- Creeping Jenny (*Lysimachia*, Zone 4)
- Deadnettle (*Lamium*, Zone 3)
- Lily-of-the-valley (*Convallaria*, Zone 2)
- Mazus (*Mazus*, Zone 4)

- Periwinkle (*Vinca*, Zone 4)
- Rock cress, snow-in-summer (*Aubretia*, Zone 4)
- Spurge (*Pachysandra*, Zone 4)
- Sweet woodruff (*Asperula odorata*, Zone 4)
- Wild ginger (*Asarum europeum*, Zones 4 to 5)
- Wintercreeper (*Euonymous*, Zone 4)
- Wintergreen or checkerberry (*Gaultheria procumbens*, Zones 3 to 4)

See also ferns, page 82, and ornamental grasses, page 79.

Ajuga reptans 'Bronze Beauty'

Biennials

Biennials live for two years. In their first, they produce foliage, and flowers appear the second summer. Some gardeners get a jump on summer's show by setting out purchased plants ready to flower; others enjoy sowing seed and the anticipation of results. Cold-climate biennials include bellflower (*Campanula medium,* Zone 3), delphinium (*D. × elatum,* Zone 2; *D. × belladonna,* Zone 3; Giant Imperial Series), foxglove (*Digitalis purpurea,* Zone 4), hollyhock (*Alcea rosea,* Zone 3), Iceland poppy (*Papaver nudicaule,* Zone 2), and sweet William (*Dianthus barbatus,* Zone 3).

Perennials hardy to Zone 4

All plants hardy to Zone 3, plus:

- Aster, *Aster*
- Bee balm, *Monarda*
- Big blue lobelia, *Lobelia*
- Boltonia, *Boltonia*
- Butterfly weed, *Asclepias*
- Coreopsis, tickseed, *Coreopsis*
- Dalmatian cranesbill and Endress's geranium, *Geranium*
- False spirea, *Astilbe*
- Joe-Pye weed, *Eupatorium*
- Lamb's-ears, *Stachys*
- Peony, *Paeonia*
- Red valerian, *Centranthus*
- Rock cress, *Aubretia*
- Shasta daisy, *Chrysanthemum*
- Snakeroot, *Cimicifuga*
- Speedwell, *Veronica*
- Spirea, *Spiraea*
- Wall rock cress, *Arabis*

Bee balm

Butterfly weed

Joe-Pye weed

BULBS

As used today, the term *bulb* refers not only to true bulbs, but often also to corms, rhizomes, and tubers. The tulip is an example of a true bulb, crocus of a corm, iris of a rhizome, and dahlia of a tuber. Leon Snyder, founding director of the University of Minnesota Landscape Arboretum and an extraordinary plantsman, succinctly described the bulb world as falling into three groups: hardy spring-flowering bulbs, planted in autumn; tender summer- and autumn-flowering bulbs, planted in spring; and hardy spring-, summer-, and autumn-flowering bulbs such as iris or daylilies that may be treated as perennials for the sunny flower border. For some bulbs, the difference between late spring and early summer, or late summer and early autumn, is a gray area.

Whatever type you may be preparing to plant, don't bother with any that have soft spots, for they aren't sound. Select only those that are firm, plump, and pleasantly dry to the touch. Exceptions are lilies and dahlia and caladium tubers; these should be kept barely moist. If you have bulbs you can't plant right away, set them in a relatively cool, dry place; again, keep those that should be moist from drying out. Holding bulbs for a few days isn't problematic. Overwintering bulbs — digging them up and storing them during their dormancy under conditions your garden cannot provide — is a different enterprise (see page 74).

Bulbs will grow in most garden soils. If your soil is excessively clayey or sandy, amend it as needed. In colder climates, autumn planting can be done after frost has occurred, but before cold has made the ground hard. September and October are fine for my area around Concord, New Hampshire (Zone 5). The timing of spring planting depends on variety, but in any case shouldn't be earlier than when the soil can be worked easily.

Don't try to plant if there has recently been lots of rain and the soil is wet. Spade the soil well to a depth of at least 18 inches. Work in some peat moss (moistened thoroughly first, but not wringing wet), sand, or vermiculite to loosen the soil if it is clay, or compost or leaf mold if it is too sandy. You may also add bone meal, at the rate of 7 pounds per 100 square feet. If you are planting bulbs that must stay moist, keep them covered with a damp cloth to shield them from drying sun and wind. When planting, a trowel or bulb planter is the tool to reach for if it's a matter of placing a few bulbs. You'll need a spade, though, to plant a large number of bulbs to be set at the same depth, in what some call a "tray

Late tulip (Tulipa tarda)

bed." Refer to a reputable gardening guide or your bulb source for the correct planting depth for your bulbs, which varies by type. When planted only a little deeper than recommended, bulbs may put off flowering for as long as 10 days to two weeks, a phenomenon you can use to advantage if you want to stagger flowering. Tamp the soil down so it's in good contact with the bulbs, and water in well.

Care of Bulbs

In winter, once the soil has frozen, mulch bulb beds with a 3- to 6-inch layer of evergreen boughs, pine bark, or straw. This will keep soil temperatures more even, helping to prevent frost heaves and premature sprouting during warm spells. Remove the mulch in spring as soon as an inch of growth is visible, but do so gently so as not to injure the shoots. You can scratch in some bone meal or 5-10-10 fertilizer at this time. Bulbs require little maintenance. Spent flowers should be removed so the plant doesn't put energy unnecessarily into producing seed. Leave the foliage and stems of spent blooms until they have turned quite brown, as they continue to help the bulb manufacture food.

Some bulbs will generate new ones, increasing their number and spreading out from the area originally planted. Bulbs that increase in this way are said to "naturalize." If bloom seems to be failing, the bulbs may have become overcrowded. Dig them up and divide the clumps, discarding any soft bulbs before replanting. Some bulbs give a splendid show their first year, but then it's downhill from there. Many tulip cultivars, unlike species (that is, naturally occurring or unimproved) tulips, don't return reliably year after year. Hyacinths too tend to decrease over the years. Daffodils will do well for years, unless they get too much water just when the bulbs are preparing for fall.

Overwintering Tender Bulbs

We are accustomed to the sight of bulbs pushing their stems up through snow crusts to bloom in earliest spring, but all bulbs are not of equal hardiness. There are tender bulbs, mostly among the summer-flowerers. Gladiolus, dahlias, and begonias are some tender bulbs that can be thought of as annuals in colder climates. Plant out dahlia tubers two weeks before your frost-free date (container-grown plants after the frost-free date). Gladiolus and begonias should be planted out after the danger of frost is past.

Lift tender bulbs just after the first frost. Discard any soft bulbs or those damaged by your spade. Keep them mold-free, yet not dried out, and safe from freezing temperatures. Some gardeners dip bulbs into captan fungicide or Benlate solution to keep disease at bay. Bulb expert John Bryan advises storing them in moistened peat moss at 40°F. Tulip bulbs should be stored in dry peat moss, those of lilies and other moist bulbs in lightly moistened peat. For corms, detach and store the new, primary cormel; discard the old, shriveled corm, and the tiny cormels too, unless you want to carry them over two more years until they are of flowering size.

Some cold-climate gardeners may not have luck growing the earliest-flowering of tulips and narcissus, due to the nasty surprise of late frost. At summer's close, early fall frosts can put a stop to the blooms of dahlia and gladiolus, so choose the early-flowering among these and other frost-tender blooms. In areas such as the plains states where hot, dry weather is typical of spring, plant bulbs where they will have some shade. Since trees may not be in leaf when the bulbs flower, the shade cast by a structure such as a building or wall will serve. Or place them among other plants that will shade them.

Thanks to the passionate interest of breeders, there are phenomenal numbers of cultivars of *Crocus, Hemerocallis, Iris, Lilium, Narcissus,* and *Tulipa.* You can read through a handful of the best and thickest catalogs and find few dupicated entries.

Hardy Spring-Flowering Bulbs
- Bluebell, English, *Hyacinthoides non-scripta,* aka *Endymion non-scriptus, Scilla non-scripta,* Zones 4 to 5
- Bluebell, Spanish, *Hyacinthoides hispanica,* Zones 3 to 4
- Crocus, *Crocus* spp., Zones 3 to 5
- Daffodil, jonquil, narcissus, *Narcissus* spp., many to Zone 3
- Dog-tooth violet, *Erythronium,* Zones 4 to 5
- European wood anemone, *Anemone nemorosa,* Zones 4 to 5
- Fritillaria, *Fritillaria* spp., Zones 3 to 5
- Glory of the snow, *Chionodoxa,* Zone 3
- Grape hyacinth, *Muscari* spp., Zones 3 to 4
- Hyacinth, *Hyacinthus orientalis,* Zones 3 to 4
- Iris, *Iris.* Crested iris, *I. cristata,* Zones 3 to 4; dwarf bearded iris, *I. pumila,* Zone 3; Japanese iris, *I. ensata,* Zone 4
- Jack-in-the-pulpit, *Arisaema,* Zones 3 to 4
- Lily-of-the-valley, *Convallaria majalis,* Zone 3
- Meadow saffron, *Colchicum luteum,* Zone 4
- Ornamental onion, *Allium,* mostly Zone 4
- Quamash, wild hyacinth, *Camassia,* Zones 3 to 4
- Siberian squill, *Scilla sibirica,* Zone 2

Narcissus

Jack-in-the-pulpit

- Snowdrop, *Galanthus* spp., Zone 3
- Spring snowflake, *Leucojum vernum,* Zones 3 to 4
- Spring starflower, *Ipheion uniflorum,* Zone 5
- Striped squill, *Puschkinia scilloides* var. *libanotica,* Zone 4
- Tulip, *Tulipa* spp. There are 15 classes of tulip and hundreds of cultivars, virtually all hardy, some to Zone 2. Among the most successful for cold-climate gardens are *Tulipa humilis,* Zone 4; *T. kaufmanniana,* Zone 4; *T. kolpakowskiana;* T. *pulchella,* Zone 4; and *T. tarda,* Zone 4
- Winter aconite, *Eranthis,* Zone 4

Hardy Summer-Flowering Bulbs

Lily

- Daylily, *Hemerocallis,* Zones 3 to 4. Hundreds upon hundreds of cultivars
- Iris, *Iris,* many hardy to Zone 3
- Lily, *Lilium.* Hundreds of excellent cultivars. The hardier types include Asiatic, Zone 4; Butterfly series, Zone 4; *L. candidum,* Zone 4; *L. martagon,* Zone 3; Turk's-cap lily, *L. superbum,* Zone 4; Trumpet, Zone 5
- Ornamental onion, *Allium* spp., many to Zone 4
- Summer snowflake, *Leucojum aestivum,* Zones 3 to 4
- Wood anemone, *Anemone sylvestris* 'Snow Drop', Zones 3 to 4

Hardy Autumn-Flowering Bulbs

Anemone

- Anemone, *Anemone hupehensis,* Zone 5; Japanese anemone, *A. japonica,* Zone 5; *A. tomentosa,* Zones 3 to 4; *A. vitifolia,* Zone 3
- Autumn crocus (meadow saffron), *Colchicum* spp., Zones 4 to 5
- Fall crocus, *Crocus* spp., Zones 4 to 5
- Ornamental onion, *Allium thunbergii,* Zone 4

Asiatic lilies: Lilium *'Corina' (orange) and 'Nove Cento' (yellow).*

CHAPTER 6

GRASSES, FERNS, AND WATER PLANTS

ORNAMENTAL GRASSES

The popularity of ornamental grasses has virtually exploded during the past 20 years, and for good reason: the versatility of these relatively fast-growing perennials in landscape use verges on the phenomenal. Some grasses are exquisite for trim edgings, some make magnificent specimen plantings. Many are handsome participants in the mixed border, others make their contribution in wet soils or even standing water. Some are good choices for ground cover, others for screens. Use them to accent the rock garden or to make your property more attractive to birds. Whether you favor naturalistic masses or elegant clumps, there are ornamental grasses to suit. Color of stem and plume seems virtually unlimited, encompassing quiet beige and blue, silver, gold and green, scarlet, rust, and exuberant stripes. Some are evergreen, some turn almost blond with a change in season.

Many of these grasses manage in windswept locations where other ornamentals would be miserable. In very exposed, windy locations, you may need to protect new plantings of marginally hardy grasses during the first winter. Provide all new plantings with ample water throughout their first growing season, well into autumn. For most, soil must be free-draining, and full sun is

A stand of feather reed grass (Calamagrostis acutiflora), *with sedum 'Autumn Joy' and black-eyed Susan* (Rudbeckia).

Grasses for Wet Soils or Water Gardens

- Arundo species
- Eulalia grass
- Feather reed grass 'Karl Foerster'
- Fountain grass species
- Giant miscanthus
- Palm sedge
- Ribbon grass 'Picta', var. *luteo-picta* and 'Feeseys Form'
- Sweet flag
- Switch grass
- Tufted hair grass

preferred, but of course there are exceptions. Happily, hardy varieties are legion.

Most are best cut to the ground in early spring, to give new growth its best shot and to avoid a ratty look by midsummer. Cut back in autumn at your peril, for most of these plants survive harsh weather better intact, and many will provide some winter interest as a dividend. Indeed, some ornamental grasses are at their most spectacular in winter, displaying a dramatic change of color or gorgeous seed heads.

Early spring is the time to plant, for then the grass will have time to establish itself before hot summer weather arrives. Spade soil well to a depth of 18 inches and clear it of weeds and stones. Amend the soil as necessary; note that most ornamental grasses aren't heavy feeders. Water the newly planted grass in well, then mulch.

Ornamental Grasses Hardy to Zone 2
- Skinners golden brome, *Bromus inermis* 'Skinners Golden'
- Sweet grass (holy grass), *Hierochloa odorata*

Ornamental Grasses Hardy to Zone 3
All grasses hardy to Zone 2, plus:
- Broomsedge, *Andropogon virginicus*
- Mountain sedge, *Carex montanensis*

Ornamental Grasses Hardy to Zone 4
All grasses hardy to Zone 3, plus:
- Big bluestem, *Andropogon gerardii*: 'Kaw', Zone 4; 'Niagra', Zone 4
- Blue oat grass, *Helictotrichon sempervirens* 'Saphirsprudel'
- Bulbous oat grass, *Arrhenatherum elatius bulbosum* 'Variegatum'
- Eastern feathergrass, *Stipa extremorientalis*
- Fall-blooming reed grass, *Calamagrostis brachytricha*
- Fescue, *Festuca amethystina* 'Bronzeglanz'; klose fesue, *F.a.* 'Klose'; *F. cinerea* (many blue cultivars); *F. ovina glauca*; hair fescue, *F. tenuifolia*
- Hakonegrass, *Hakonechloa macra* 'Aureola'

Big bluestem

- Indian grass, *Sorghastrum avenaceum*, *S. nutans* 'Holt', 'Osage', and 'Rumsey'
- Japanese themeda, *Themeda triandra* 'Japonica'
- Little bluestem, *Schizachyrium scoparium*
- Miscanthus (Eulalia grass, Japanese silver grass), *Miscanthus sinensis* 'Gracilimus', 'Malepartus', and 'Purpurascens'
- Moorgrass, *Sesleria:* blue moorgrass, *S. caerulea;* green moorgrass, *S. heufleriana;* gray moorgrass, *S. nitida*
- Mosquito grass, *Bouteloua gracilis*
- Prairie dropseed, *Sporobolus heterolepis*
- Purple moor grass, *Molinia caerulea* subsp. *arundinacea* 'Bergfreund', 'Skyracer', 'Staefa', 'Transparent', and 'Windspiel'
- Ravenna grass, *Erianthus ravennae*
- Ribbon grass, *Phalaris arundinacea*
- Sedge, *Carex:* black sedge, *C. nigra;* blue sedge, *C. flacca;* finger sedge, *C. digitata;* Gray's sedge, *C. grayi;* palm sedge, *C. muskingumensis;* variegated palm sedge, *C.m.* 'Oehme'
- Sideoats gramma, *Bouteloua curtipendula*
- Sweet flag, *Acorus calamus*, variegated sweet flag, *A.c.* 'Variegatus'
- Switch grass, *Panicum virgatum*
- Tufted hair grass, *Deschampsia caspitosa*
- Yellow foxtail grass, *Alopecurus pratensis aureus*

Ornamental Grasses Hardy to Zone 5
All grasses hardy to Zone 4, plus:
- Arundo, *Arundo formosana* 'Green Fountain'
- Big bluestem, *Andropogon gerardii:* 'Sentinel'

Miscanthus (Miscanthus sinensis 'Silver Feather') is spectacular in winter; the large plumes catch the sun, and the stems show starkly against a backdrop of snow.

Indian grass

- Feather reed grass, *Calamagrostis* × *acutiflora*
- Fescue, *Festuca amethystina,* large blue fescue
- Fountain grass, *Pennisetum alopecuroides* 'Little Honey'
- Japanese blood grass, *Imperata cylindrica* 'Red Baron'
- Japanese sedge, *Carex morrowii:* 'Aurea-variegata', 'Old Gold', and 'Variegata'
- Miscanthus (Eulalia grass, Japanese silver grass), *Miscanthus: sinensis* 'Adagio', 'Blutenwunder', 'Ferner Osten', 'Kirk Alexander', 'Morning Light'; giant miscanthus, *M. floridulus*
- Quaking grass, *Briza media*

Fountain grass

FERNS

Ferns contribute a sedate quality to the garden. Fairly quick of growth, they can make the planting they grace seem deceptively mature. When admiring a garden that includes ferns, one often has the impression that it is tended by a capable, sophisticated gardener. If this isn't always precisely the case, we have the easygoing nature of many ferns to thank.

With sufficient shade and moist, free-draining soil, many hardy ferns will thrive. Some can tolerate more sun than others. Planting in spring gives the root system the longest time possible to get established before the arrival of really cold weather. If planting on a hot, sunny day is unavoidable, take great care to protect the vulnerable fern. Water in your new transplant generously, and don't let the soil around it get very dry until the fern is established in its new location. Some ferns must never be allowed to get very thirsty. As you would for most other new plantings, water thoroughly throughout the first spring and summer, right into autumn. To slow evaporation of moisture from the soil (and keep down competition from weeds), fern expert John Mickel recommends a mulch of wood chips and leaves — don't forget to shred the leaves before spreading them — or buckwheat hulls and cocoa shells.

Give ferns some windbreak if planting in a location exposed to stiff winds, for the fronds are somewhat brittle. Ferns as a group are surprisingly varied. Some grow well in sunny locations, others in swampy soil. They may be minute, or 6-foot giants. Some are evergreen. A sampling of the hardiest and least temperamental ferns follows.

Five-finger maidenhair fern (Adiantum *spp.*)

Lady fern

Wood fern

Ferns Hardy to Zone 2

- Bladder fern (brittle bladder fern, fragile fern), *Cystopteris* spp.
- Flowering fern, *Osmunda:* cinnamon fern, *O. cinnamomea;* interrupted fern, *O. claytoniana;* royal fern, flowering fern, *O. regalis; O. × ruggi, O. claytoniana × regalis* var. *spectabilis*
- Lady fern, *Athyrium* spp.
- Maiden fern, *Thelypteris* spp.
- Maidenhair fern, *Adiantum* spp.
- Oak fern, *Gymnocarpium* spp.
- Ostrich fern (shuttlecock fern), *Matteuccia* spp.
- Sensitive fern (bead fern), *Onoclea* spp.
- Wood fern (shield fern, Buckler fern), *Dryopteris* spp.

Ferns Hardy to Zone 3

All ferns hardy to Zone 2, plus:
- Bracken, *Pteridium* spp.
- Hay-scented fern (boulder fern), *Dennstaedtia*
- Holly fern, *Polystichum* spp.

Ferns Hardy to Zone 4

All ferns hardy to Zone 3, plus:
- Glade fern (narrow-leaved spleenwort), *Diplazium*
- Japanese beech fern, *Thelypteris*
- Netted chain fern, *Woodwardia areolata* syn. *Lorinseria areolata*
- Nevada wood fern (Sierra water fern), *Thelypteris*
- New York fern (tapering fern), *Thelypteris*
- Silvery spleenwort (silvery glade fern), *Athyrium*
- Slender fragile fern, *Cystopteris*
- Upside-down fern, *Arachniodes*

Ferns Hardy to Zone 5

All ferns hardy to Zone 4, plus:
- Fendler's lip fern, *Cheilanthes*

Ferns Happy in Wet Soil

- Cinnamon fern, *Osmunda cinnamomea*
- Lady fern, *Athyrium filix-femina*
- Marsh fern, *Thelypteris*
- Royal or flowering fern, *Osmunda regalis*
- Sensitive or bead fern, *Onoclea sensibilis*

- Hard fern (deer fern), *Blechnum*
- Holly fern, *Cyrtomium*
- Lady fern, crenate, *Athyrium*

WATER GARDEN PLANTS AND MARGINALS

Marginal plants grow in shallow standing water or in soil that is always wet. Tender water garden plants make expensive annuals (although with some trouble they can be lifted and overwintered in good-sized containers in a frost-free location), but happily, there is a broad selection of pond and marginal plants hardy in colder climates. New and interesting introductions come along regularly, so if you are a water-garden enthusiast, you'll enjoy looking through up-to-date catalogs from time to time. Plants of the genus *Nymphaea,* the water lilies, have been the most conspicuously bred, followed by lotuses. Some of these represent a considerable financial investment, so it's wise to ask any questions you may have about a particular plant before placing your order. Aquatic plant expert and grower Greg Speichert (Crystal Palace Perennials, St. John, Indiana) points out that many of the hardy lotus may not bloom in areas with cool summers. See also grasses for wet locations, page 80; ferns for wet locations, page 84; and lobelia.

Hardy Water Plants
- Lotus, *Lotus.* Many hardy to Zone 4
- Water lilies, *Nymphaea* spp. Many hardy to Zone 3

Marginal Plants Hardy to Zone 3
- Blue flag, *Iris versicolor.* Some are hardy.
- Button bush, *Cephalanthus*
- Cattails, *Typha*
- Flowering rush, *Butomus*
- Hardy water wisteria, *Hygrophila*
- Northern calla lily, *Calla*
- Pink butterfly plant, *Asclepias*
- Rush, *Juncus*
- Water baby's breath, *Alisma*

Water lilies

Marginal Plants Hardy to Zone 4

All water plants hardy to Zone 3, plus:

- Arrowhead (duck potato), *Sagittaria*
- Golden creeping Jenny, *Lysimachia*
- Hardy umbrella grass, *Cyperus*
- Horsetails (scouring rush), *Equisetum*
- Marsh marigold, *Caltha*
- Reed, *Phragmites australis*
- Rush, *Scirpus*
- Swamp candles, *Lysimachia*
- Variegated manna grass, *Glyceria*
- Water willow, *Justicia*
- White water buttercup, *Ranunculus*
- Yellow flag, *Iris pseudacorus*

Hardy umbrella grass

Marginal Plants Hardy to Zone 5

All water plants hardy to Zone 4, plus:

- Golden lanterns, *Lysimachia*
- *Houttuynia cordata*
- Lizard tail, *Saururus*
- Mint, aquatic and brook, *Mentha*
- Pennywort, *Hydrocotyle*
- Pickerel weed, *Pontederia*
- Sweet flag, *Acorus* spp.
- Tufts of gold, *Lysimachia*
- Water arum, *Peltandra*
- Water clover, *Marsilea*
- Water forget-me-not, *Myosotis scorpioides*

Marsh marigold

Yellow flag iris

CHAPTER 7

ROSES THAT CAN TAKE THE COLD

Roses vary widely in hardiness. Many, but not all, shrub roses are hardy — and the more shrub roses are hybridized, the more tender roses are brought into the shrub rose gene pool. Some old garden roses — Albas, Centifolias, Damasks, Gallicas, Hybrid Spinosissimas, Moss roses — are hardy, some are not. Hybridization has resulted in the notably hardy roses of the Griffith Buck, Explorer, Morden, and Parkland series. Generalizations can be made about the hardiness of rose classes, but because there are many exceptions, it is wise to ask about the hardiness of a rose before purchasing it.

Hardier Rose Classes	Less Hardy Rose Classes
Species	Moss
Centifolia	Damask
Eglanteria	Damask Perpetual
Gallica	Rambler
Hybrid Rugosa	Noisette
Hybrid Spinosissima	Polyantha
	Hybrid Tea
	Floribunda
	Grandiflora
	Large-flowered Climber
	China

'Charles Lawson'

Ten of the Most Popular Hardy Roses

- 'John Cabot' (Explorer; Shrub)
- 'Hansa' (Hybrid Rugosa)
- 'Blanc Double de Coubert' (Hybrid Rugosa)
- 'The Fairy' (Polyantha Shrub)
- 'Stanwell Perpetual' (Hybrid Spinosissima)
- 'Queen Elizabeth' (Grandiflora)
- 'Betty Prior' (Floribunda)
- 'Bonica' (Shrub)
- 'Mister Lincoln' (Hybrid Tea)
- *Rosa mundi* (Shrub)

'Blanc Double de Coubert' (Hybrid Rugosa)

There are roses that grow on their own roots, and then there are budded roses, which are grafted onto a hardier rootstock. The graft union of a rose can be a weak spot; it will die of cold before the roots. That is why own-root roses are generally more cold-resistant. In Zones 3 to 5, it is easier to grow own-root roses, and they flourish better. If you don't know whether a rose is growing on its own roots when you buy it, look for the graft union, a swelling of the stem several inches above the roots.

PLANTING ROSES

Obtain only #1 grade plants (those with at least three good canes). When buying a rose, avoid plants with any sign of disease. Avoid those with new shoots and leaves, too, as it's much preferable to plant dormant roses. Make certain the canes are green; you may need to scrape them a bit with a fingernail to check. Cold-climate gardeners may have disappointing results with packaged roses, and not only because they can't be examined thoroughly before purchase. Many of the packaged roses for sale in the northern United States are unsold

Should You Plant Roses in Fall?

Though it's common to plant roses in spring, it isn't always possible. Rose expert and hybridizer Malcolm ("Mike") Lowe, who has propagated thousands of roses in Nashua, New Hampshire, has had such good results with fall planting as to put the dictum of spring planting into question. (Remember that this applies to *cold* climates.) He finds that roses planted in fall after the first frost fare extremely well. This is because the rose is pushed into full dormancy. And fall planting encourages the rose to set a good root system, resulting in a better plant. Strip off the foliage, trim the rose back, plant it, and cover it with a protective styrofoam Rose Kone. Mike has fall-planted 1,000 roses this way, losing only three. He says this autumn technique holds to Zone 3, and into November. So don't panic if the rose you've been dreaming about finally shows up on your doorstep in autumn. If the plant is dormant, you should have no problem.

merchandise offered months earlier in the South, and many of these roses have been damaged by improper storage during their time "on the shelf" and in shipping.

Give a new rose an excellent environment in which to grow. A location with at least six hours of sun per day is essential. The soil should be loose and have plenty of organic matter. You can work in well-rotted cow or horse manure when planting. Prepare a 30-inch planting hole. If you can manage only something like 24 inches, for whatever reason, angle the rose so both the bud union and the roots are at the desired depth. That will spread out the root system. In growing, the rose will correct the angle both above and below the soil. Plant own-root roses at the same depth as they were in their container. In cold climates, the graft union of a budded rose should be planted 2 to 4 inches below soil level, where it will be better insulated against cold; the colder the winters, the deeper the graft union should be situated. Before planting a bare-root rose, prune away any dead, diseased, or soft tissue. Remove all but the three strongest canes and trim them to about 5 inches long. Then submerge the plant in water for as long as 24 hours to rehydrate it.

Fully dormant roses are best prepared to survive winter. Roses that aren't fully dormant are more likely to suffer damage and winterkill. In colder climates rose canes of even hardy roses can suffer winter injury, which may range from dieback at the tips to losing canes, or even dieback to the crown. Snow is an effective insulator against winterkill; where there is good and constant snow cover, canes may die back to the snow line, yet the portions below that point come through with flying colors.

'Chuckles'

Prepare Your Roses for Winter

Rosarian Mike Lowe puts a Rose Kone in place in preparation for winter's worst; the canes of the rose have been shortened only slightly, not drastically cut back.

If a rose has very long canes that are likely to whip about in strong winds and damage the plant, shorten them modestly. Even though you'll need to remove winterkill come spring, the plants will be considerably larger and have many more blooms than if they'd been cut way back. For heavy protection, Mike places a Rose Kone with the tip cut off (or stacks two, as a double layer) over the plant. If the rose extends much above the top of the cone — and if he wants to protect that portion of the canes — he wraps the exposed canes in a couple of layers of plastic burlap, up to a height of as much as 40 inches. A double layer of Rose Kones can be used for even more insulation. Moderate protection consists of a Rose Kone, nothing more. For very large plants such as climbers, Mike constructs a box from an insulating board such as Homosauet; canes can be tucked down into the protective box.

PROTECTION

The first step is to make sure your roses go into winter fully dormant. Although there are many handsome garden roses that will flourish in Zones 3, 4, and 5 without protection, many more can do so with some protection. One simple way to protect roses from damaging temperature changes is to use mulch. Mulch increases insulation and helps prevent frost heaves. Maintain a mulch depth of 3 to 4 inches year round, but keep mulch from touching the canes and crown, for cold, wet material against the rose will damage it. Another easy protective step

The extent of winterkill can be evaluated when the protection is removed in spring.

is to apply an antidesiccant in spring and autumn to keep moisture loss and the resulting damage at a minimum.

To help your roses acclimate for winter, that is, go fully dormant, don't apply any fertilizer after mid-August, so the rose won't push out lots of tender, new growth. Mike Lowe recommends breaking off the top 2 to 3 inches of new growth from budless canes at summer's end. Some tender, new growth will probably occur (and be killed over the winter), but doing this causes the rest of the cane to harden up. Also, although deadheading of spent blooms is important throughout the early and middle parts of the summer to encourage repeat bloom and to clean up the plants, don't deadhead after August 1. When blooms develop into hips, that is a cue for the rose to begin preparations for dormancy. Another of Mike's tricks is to persuade the varietal top portion of a budded rose to send out some roots, which will strengthen the plant: When planting, scratch your fingernail into the bark, right into the cambium, above the bud union, and dust on some rooting hormone powder. With luck, roses will push out additional, own (of the budded variety) roots.

Roses that need extra winter insulation are more vulnerable to drying wind than to cold. Few gardeners can count on snow cover to shelter roses. Of the protective plant covers commercially sold for roses, styrofoam Rose Kones are chosen by many professional cold-climate rose growers over waxed cardboard cones and collars, which are less effective insulators. Don't try to "insulate" roses with peat moss, mulch, or leaves; not only can the fill encourage disease, but when it gets wet, it is death to rose canes.

ROSE CARE

Feed roses in early spring and after each period of bloom — never in fall! At spring planting time, apply an organic (nonchemical) fertilizer. For established roses, a chemical fertilizer relatively high in phosphorus will encourage a large, vigorous root system; the exact formulation of fertilizer will depend on which of the essential nutrients (N, nitrogen; P, phosphorus; K, potassium) your soil lacks for growing good roses. It is best to have soil samples analyzed before embarking on a program of chemical fertilizer. Avoid urea-based fertilizers, as they burn rose tissue. Apply fertilizer away from the crown and canes of the rose. Replenish mulch as it wears away. Mulch keeps weeds down and conserves moisture. If an amendment such as well-rotted cow manure is used for mulch, it will feed your roses, too.

To read more, see the publication cited on page 113 describing the excellent research conducted on 85 hardy roses by the Minnesota Agricultural Experiment Station.

AN EXPERT'S SELECTION:
40 of Mike Lowe's Favorite Roses for Cold Climates

'Great Maiden's Blush'	Alba
Rosa 'Alba Semiplena', White Rose of York	Alba
'Charles Lawson'	Bourbon (Hybrid Bourbon)
Rosa centifolia	Centifolia
'Jeanne Lajoie'	Climbing Miniature
'Nozomi'	Climbing Miniature
'Blush Damask'	Damask
'Celsiana'	Damask
'Mme. Hardy'	Damask
'Marie Louise'	Damask
'Omar Khayyam'	Damask
'Greenmantle'	Eglanteria
'Chuckles'	Floribunda
'Charles de Mills'	Gallica
'Jenny Duval'	Gallica
Rosa gallica var. *officinalis*	Gallica
R. gallica versicolor	Gallica
'Mme. Plantier'	Hybrid Alba
'Seven Sisters', *R. multiflora platyphylla*	Hybrid Multiflora
'Charles Lefebvre'	Hybrid Perpetual
'Enfant de France'	Hybrid Perpetual
'Baltimore Belle'	Hybrid Setigera
'William Baffin'	Kordesii
'Clair Matin'	Large-flowered Climber
'Flammentanz'	Large-flowered Climber

'Hansa' (Hybrid Rugosa)

'Long John Silver'	Large-flowered Climber
'New Dawn'	Large-flowered Climber
Rosa × centifolia 'Muscosa'	Moss
'Comtesse de Murinais' (White Moss)	Moss (best white)
'Louis Gimard'	Moss (best pink)
'William Lobb'	Moss (best lavender)
'Lullaby'	Polyantha
'Rose-Marie Viaud'	Rambler
'Autumn Sunset'	Shrub
'Dornroschen' ('Sleeping Beauty')	Shrub
'Immortal Juno'	Shrub
'Lilian Austin'	Shrub
Rosa multiflora nana 'The Gift'	Polyantha
Rosa arvensis 'Splendens'	Species
Rosa moyesii	Species

CHAPTER 8
HARDY SHRUBS AND TREES

Shrubs and trees give structure to the landscape. They provide safe haven for beast and bird, and privacy for people. They offer the much-needed windbreaks so important in a colder climate, and control erosion on sloping terrain. If trees provide majesty of scale, shrubs bring the beauty to a human level. Together they may constitute the garden itself or provide a backdrop so other features are the focus. Many gardens rely on a handful of specimen trees or shrubs in their schemes, so it can be devastating to lose a key plant to bitter weather. Such a loss leaves a hole in the picture, and it takes years to bring along a replacement to handsome maturity. Make your selection thoughtfully, for you are investing in the future.

Choose shrubs and trees with a good track record of survival in your area. Consider native plants, for they are at home in the conditions and the sort of situation you can probably offer them. Which is likely to create a more gorgeous impression: a native in its full glory, or an import struggling to survive? Before making a purchase, travel about and make note of candidates you like. Gardening neighbors are naturally a good source of information, as are local parks, protected lands, and, should you be so fortunate as to find them nearby,

Malus *'Selkirk' achieves a stunning spring display.*

Choose Plants for Fall and Winter Beauty

Many trees and shrubs boast evergreen foliage, interesting bark, or stunning form once leaves have dropped, any of which can be an asset to the cold-climate garden. Foliage color in gold, gold-green, silver-blue, blue, blue-green, silver-green, gray-green, purple-red, and others all offer terrific accents to the green background of the garden picture; by thoughtfully weaving in some of these standouts, you can enjoy stunning variety in foliage color and texture.

---

arboreta. Commercial nurseries, on the other hand, may not give impartial advice. When you inquire about an appealing plant at one of your local nurseries, you may be told that "with a little extra care," or "with protection," the shrub or tree will flourish. Find out what this "care" entails, and describe to the nurseryman the location you have in mind for the plant. Remember, backed by the wall of a building and with a favorable exposure, a plant *may* be protected enough to survive a typical winter in a location that might otherwise be too cold. But how will it do out in the landscape? Many nurseries routinely carry plants that are marginally hardy for the area, and it takes discipline not to want to bring them all home.

Give your new shrub or tree a good planting situation, where it will have the growing space, air circulation, and type of soil and sunlight it requires. Some of the broadleaf evergreens, for instance, do better with some protection from strong sunlight in the dead of winter, and appreciate filtered or dappled light. A fine-needled evergreen would manage better than a rhododendron in an exposed, wind-battered site. Many shrubs achieve their prettiest form when sited out of the path of strong northerly or westerly winds. Virtually all trees and shrubs thrive in well-drained soils. If the site you have your heart set on seems acceptable but for poor drainage, work in enough organic soil amendment to improve it; your new plant won't survive in standing water.

If you are the one bringing home your selection, do so with care. If it is so large you need to transport it in a car with the tailgate open or in the bed of a truck, protect the plant from windburn, which can occur even at the seemingly sedate speed of 35 mph. Some commercial growers treat foliage with antidesic-

Burning bush (Euonymous alatus), *fall color*

cant when moving plants on sunny, hot, or windy days. Avoid planting on bright, scorching days when a vulnerable transplant is at the mercy of drying sun and exhausting heat; overcast and even damp days are much less stressful for a plant moving to a new home. Protect the roots from drying and prune off any damaged or soft root tissue.

PLANTING TREES AND SHRUBS

Early spring is best; a good rule of thumb is to plant when forsythia blooms. Spring planting gives the new arrival the maximum time to settle into its new location and get on with the business of good growth before cold weather slows

Variegated euonymous (Euonymous fortunei *'Emerald 'n' Gold'*)

progress to a crawl. This is especially true of bare-root purchases, which need prompt attention as soon as they are in your care; soak the roots and lower stems for at least 12 hours and then plant. Shrubs can be planted in early fall as well as early spring. But whatever the season you plant, make sure the soil is at least 45°F and loose. Some experts spray foliage with an antidesiccant to help the plant survive the shock of transplantation. Water thoroughly in the days following planting and amply throughout the first growing season.

FERTILIZER

The time to give a tree a chemical fertilizer is when it can use it, meaning when the roots are active. Deciduous trees put on growth fairly evenly over the summer, as do the evergreens arborvitae, hemlock, and yew. Other evergreens put on a sort of growth spurt at summer's outset, and thereafter just the roots keep at it throughout the season. Shrubs should be fertilized every spring, when they begin active growth. If you use a commercially prepared fertilizer for trees and shrubs, select a balanced formula (1:1:1) unless there is a soil deficiency you are trying to improve. You want to avoid promoting lots of new, tender growth late in the season, with bitter weather just around the corner. Most experts agree that this means no chemical or other liquid fertilizer (such as manure tea) later than mid-August. A solid organic fertilizer, which requires some time to break down before the plant can use it, may be applied in late autumn; it will have all winter and early spring to rot nicely. A slow-release fertilizer is acceptable in late summer or autumn.

MULCH

Apply mulch when planting a tree or shrub, and renew the layer to a depth of several inches in autumn to protect the roots from frost heaves. Experts at the University of New Hampshire Cooperative Extension recommend a 10- to 12-inch layer of dry leaf mulch or pine needles, bark, or weathered wood chips to a depth of 2 to 3 inches. Keep mulch at least 2 inches away from the stems of shrubs susceptible to early frost damage, such as azaleas. Mulch moderates soil temperature, reduces moisture loss in summer, and discourages the growth of weeds. It keeps the ground unfrozen for as long as possible, so water in the soil remains available to the plant.

> ## Street Trees
>
> If you wish to plant a tree or shrub near a roadway, make sure it's a salt-tolerant plant. Salt and salty sand don't simply lie in the melting snow, but are splashed and sprayed by traffic a surprising distance. Avoid speckled alder, arborvitae, ash, aspen, basswood, beech, birch (European, gray, paper, or white), box elder, elm, fir, hawthorn, hemlock, American hornbeam, larch, linden, any maple, white pine, Lombardy poplar, serviceberry, or spruce.

PRUNING

Judicious pruning is important for many garden shrubs and trees to encourage and direct growth, to remove rubbing branches, to thin the plant to lessen wind resistance, to maintain shape, and to renovate a plant. First, remove any dead, diseased, or damaged branches. Dead or weakened branches can encourage pests and disease, and branches torn free by winter winds can damage their neighbors. Next, prune as necessary to encourage a more pleasing shape or fuller growth, to keep plants in bounds as necessary, and to remove any branches that cross or rub. Call a licensed arborist or tree surgeon to remove limbs you aren't able to reach easily; an inexperienced amateur shouldn't balance on a ladder and try to make these cuts.

Most trees are best pruned in early spring, as early as February. Trees of marginal hardiness should not be pruned in late autumn or early winter; autumn

Choose Hedge Plants Carefully

No one could argue the beauty of a well-grown hedge. Realize, though, that the loss of individuals in your uniform row will leave gaping holes that take years to fill in, and a gap-toothed hedge doesn't have the suave appeal of a perfect one. Give careful thought to the hardiness of the plants you are tempted to use in a hedge. If you intend your hedge to border your property, plant it far enough away from the debilitating spray of salt trucks and winter traffic.

pruning wouldn't allow time for the wound to heal before severe cold sets in, which might injure the tree. And autumn pruning can remove protective cover and leave some thin-barked trees more susceptible to sunscald (see page 8). Trees that exude sap in spring should be pruned in summer; among these are beech, birch, elm, and of course maple. You can prune shrubs in early spring, but be careful not to do your routine pruning on flowering shrubs or trees after they've produced buds for next year's flowers; prune very early bloomers after they bloom, and late bloomers as early in spring as possible. In spring you will be able to see whether your plants have suffered any winterkill, which you should then remove. Consult a good pruning manual, and you will probably have sturdier, healthier plants with little effort on your part.

PREPARING FOR WINTER

Inspect your shrubs and trees throughout the year for signs of disease and pests. Be sure your plants have sufficient moisture in autumn; this is part of your insurance against winterburn. Weekly deep watering is recommended during the first growing season for trees and shrubs.

Wrap susceptible shrubs when very cold nighttime temperatures seem imminent. Treat trees vulnerable to sunscald (page 8). Erect snow frames to protect plants such as rhododendrons and flat-topped hedges from damage by heavy, wet snow. Looking rather like teepees or sawhorses, snow frames support the weight of dense snow, which if left to accumulate on the branches of the plant could suddenly prove too much for the branches, tearing or breaking them all the way down to the ground. Trees and shrubs with multiple leaders can collect heavy snow that can tear limbs; some gardeners restrict themselves to plants that produce a single leader for that reason. You can try to brush accumulating snow off susceptible branches (if you can reach them) during a heavy snowfall, but be gentle. Branches are brittle in winter.

Arborvitae (Thuja occidentalis *'Nana Aurea'*)

The lists that follow suggest substantially hardy shrubs and trees. A range of hardiness zones is given in cases where the species of a genus vary considerably in their tolerance of cold. Before buying, it's important to check whether the plant you want is appropriate for your hardiness zone. Consult your nursery, county extension office, or preferred horticultural reference for in-depth descriptions of the plants so that you can make an informed choice. After all, you and your garden are banking on an investment of at least a few, and perhaps many, years with a new shrub or tree. One person may see the characteristics of a particular shrub or tree as a pleasure, another as a nuisance. The locust, for example, offers pods of unusual interest, but will they seem as beguiling when you are raking them up?

EVERGREEN TREES AND SHRUBS

- Arborvitae, *Thuja occidentalis*, Zone 3
- Douglas-fir, *Pseudotsuga menziesii*, Zone 4
- False cypress, *Chamaecyparis* spp., Zones 3 to 5
- Fir, *Abies* spp., Zones 2 to 5
- Heaths, *Erica* spp., Zones 4 to 5
- Heather, *Calluna vulgaris*, Zones 4 to 5
- Hemlock, *Tsuga canadensis*, Zones 2 to 4
- Juniper, *Juniperus* spp., Zones 2 to 5
- Peashrub (Siberian pea tree), *Caragana* spp., Zone 2
- Pines, *Pinus* spp., Zones 2 to 4
- Siberian carpet cypress, *Microbiota decussata*, Zones 2 to 3
- Spruce, *Picea* spp., Zones 2 to 4
- Yew, *Taxus* spp., Zones 3 to 5

False cypress

BROADLEAF EVERGREENS

- Bearberry, *Arctostaphylos uva-ursi*, Zone 2
- Bog rosemary, *Andromeda polifolia*, Zone 3
- Boxwood, *Buxus* spp., Zones 5 to 6
- Daphne, *Daphne*, Zone 5
- Euonymous, *Euonymous fortunei* 'Sun Spot', Zone 5
- Holly, *Ilex* × *meserveae* Blue Series, Zone 5
- Labrador tea, *Ledum groenlandicum*, Zone 3
- Leucothoe, *Leucothoe fontanesiana*, Zone 5
- Mountain andromeda, *Pieris floribunda*, Zone 4
- Mountain laurel, *Kalmia latifolia*, Zone 5
- Pieris, *Pieris floribunda* × *japonica* hybrids, Zone 5
- Rhododendron: see box on page 107
- Trailing arbutus (mayflower), *Epigaea repens*, Zone 2

Bearberry

Daphne

Euonymous

Mountain laurel

DECIDUOUS TREES

- Alder, *Alnus* spp., Zones 3 to 4
- Amur cork tree, *Phellodendron amurense*, Zone 4

Rhododendrons and Azaleas

Give these plants protection from drying wind and baking sun, and ensure plenty of water. Free-draining soil rich in organic matter and slightly on the acid side is best. Prune directly after flowering. Among the hardier species and introductions are:

- *Rhododendron* ssp., Zone 4: 'Girard's Yellow Pompom', 'My Mary', 'Jericho', 'Aglo', 'Henry's Red', 'Olga Mezitt'
- *Rhododendron canadense,* Rhodora, Zones 2 to 3
- *Rhododendron carolinianum × dauricum* 'PJM', Zone 4
- Rosebay rhododendron (great laurel), *Rhododendron maximum,* Zone 4; *R. ponticum* 'Roseum', Zone 5
- Korean azalea (Manchurian azalea), *Rhododendron mucronulatum,* Zone 5; 'Cornell Pink', Zone 4
- Pinkshell azalea, *Rhododendron vaseyi,* Zone 4
- *Rhododendron yakushimanum* 'Yaku Princess', Zone 4

- Notably hardy azaleas include 'Joseph Hill' (Zone 5), variegated (Zone 5), 'Pink Pancake' (-10°F), 'Rosebud' (Zone 5), 'White Rosebud' (Zone 5), and the Robin Hill Series azaleas, to Zone 3: 'Conversation Piece', 'Gillie', 'Jeanne Weeks', 'La Belle Helene', 'Lady Louise', 'Lady Robin', 'Nancy of Robin Hill', 'Watchet', and 'White Moon'. Also 'Deep Rose', Zone 4; 'Frank Abbott', Zone 4; 'Golden Showers', Zone 4; 'Jane Abbott Pink', Zone 4; 'Lemon Drop', Zone 3; 'Lollipop', Zone 4; 'Magic', Zone 4; 'Millennium', Zone 4; and 'Sparkler', Zone 4

- Ash, *Fraxinus* spp., Zones 3 to 5
- Beech, *Fagus* spp., Zones 3 to 5
- Birch, *Betula* spp., Zones 2 to 3
- Black gum (tupelo), *Nyssa sylvatica,* Zone 4
- Black locust, *Robinia pseudoacacia,* Zone 4
- Crabapple, *Malus* spp., Zones 2 to 4
- Devil's walking stick, *Aralia spinosa,* Zone 4
- Elm, *Ulmus* spp., Zones 2 to 5
- Flowering almond, *Prunus triloba,* Zone 4
- Hackberry, *Celtis occidentalis,* Zone 3
- Hazelnut, *Corylus* spp., Zones 3 to 5
- Honey locust, *Gleditsia* spp., Zone 5
- Hornbeam, *Carpinus caroliniana,* Zones 2 to 3
- Horse chestnut, *Aesculus hippocastanum,* Zones 3 to 5
- Katsura tree, *Cercidiphyllum japonicum,* Zone 4

Beech

Birch

American mountain ash (Sorbus Americana)

Malus

Serviceberry

- Larch, *Larix* spp., Zones 2 to 3
- Linden, *Tilia* spp., Zones 3 to 4
- Magnolia, *Magnolia* spp., Zone 5
- Maple, *Acer* spp., Zones 2 to 4
- Maidenhair tree, *Gingko biloba,* Zones 4 to 5
- Mountain ash, *Sorbus* spp., Zones 2 to 4
- Oak, *Quercus* spp., Zones 3 to 5
- Ohio buckeye, *Aesculus glabra,* Zone 3
- Pagoda dogwood, *Cornus alternifolia,* Zones 3 to 4
- Peking cotoneaster, *Cotoneaster acutifolius,* Zone 3
- Planetree, *Platanus* spp., Zones 4 to 5
- Poplar, *Populus* spp., Zones 1 to 4
- Russian olive, *Elaeagnus angustifolia,* Zones 2 to 3
- Serviceberry, *Amelanchier* spp., Zones 2 to 4
- Shagbark hickory, *Carya ovata,* Zone 4
- Siberian pear, *Pyrus ussuriensis,* Zones 2 to 3
- Tulip tree (yellow poplar), *Liriodedron tulipifera,* Zone 5
- Walnut, *Juglans* spp., Zones 3 to 5
- Willow, *Salix* spp., Zones 2 to 3
- Zelkova, *Zelkova serrata,* Zones 4 to 5

Maidenhair tree

Zelkova

DECIDUOUS SHRUBS

- Barberry, *Berberis thunbergii,* Zone 4
- Bayberry, *Myrica pensylvanica,* Zones 3 to 4
- Beautybush, *Kolkwitzia amabilis,* Zone 4
- Buckeye, *Aesculus* spp., Zone 4
- Burning bush, *Euonymous alatus,* Zone 4
- Butterfly bush, *Buddleia davidii,* Zone 5
- Chokeberry, *Aronia* spp., Zone 2
- Cotoneaster, *Cotoneaster* spp., Zones 4 to 5
- Daphne, *Daphne* spp., Zones 4 to 5
- Dogwood, *Cornus* spp., Zones 2 to 5
- Elderberry, *Sambucus* spp., Zone 4
- Forsythia, *Forsythia* spp., Zones 3 to 4
- Fothergilla, *Fothergilla* spp., Zones 4 to 5
- Hawthorn, *Crataegus* spp., Zones 2 to 5
- Honeysuckle, *Lonicera* spp., Zones 3 to 5
- Hydrangea, *Hydrangea* spp.: peegee hydrangea, *H. paniculata,* Zones 4 to 5; oakleaf hydrangea, *H. quercifolia,* Zone 5
- Lilac, *Syringa* spp., Zones 2 to 4
- Mock orange, *Philadelphus* spp., Zone 4
- Ninebark, *Physcarpus opulifolius,* Zone 3
- Potentilla (shrubby cinquefoil), *Potentilla fruticosa,* Zone 2
- Privet, *Ligustrum* spp., Zones 4 to 5
- Rose: see page 89
- Sea buckthorn (sallow thorn), *Hippophae rhamnoides,* Zone 4
- Silverberry, *Elaeagnus commutata,* Zone 2
- Smoke tree, *Cotinus coggygria,* Zone 5
- Spirea, *Spiraea* spp., Zones 4 to 5
- Sumac, *Rhus* spp., Zones 3 to 4
- Summersweet (sweet pepperbush), *Clethra alnifolia,* Zone 4
- Symphoricarpos (snowberry), *Symphoricarpos* spp., Zones 3 to 4
- Viburnum, *Viburnum* spp., Zones 2 to 5
- Weigela (cardinal flower), *Weigela florida,* Zone 4
- Willow, *Salix* spp., Zones 3 to 4
- Winterberry, *Ilex verticillata,* Zone 4
- Witch hazel, *Hamamelis* spp., Zones 4 to 5

Bearberry

Fothergilla

Spirea

Summersweet

HARDINESS ZONE MAP

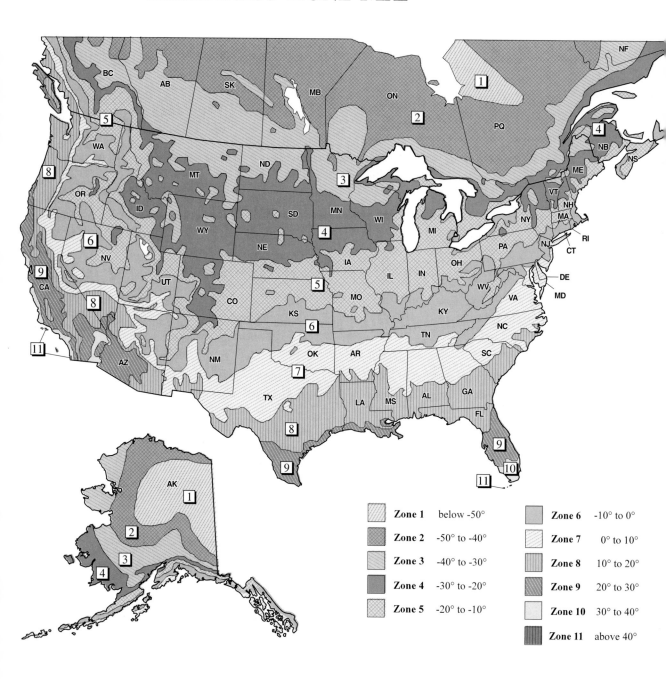

Zone 1	below -50°	**Zone 6**	-10° to 0°
Zone 2	-50° to -40°	**Zone 7**	0° to 10°
Zone 3	-40° to -30°	**Zone 8**	10° to 20°
Zone 4	-30° to -20°	**Zone 9**	20° to 30°
Zone 5	-20° to -10°	**Zone 10**	30° to 40°
		Zone 11	above 40°

FURTHER READING

Armitage, Allan M. *Herbaceous Perennial Plants*. Athens, Georgia: Varsity Press, Inc., 1989.

Barton, Barbara J. *Gardening by Mail*. Boston, Massachusetts: Houghton Mifflin Company, 1997.

Bennett, Jennifer. *The New Northern Gardener*. Buffalo, New York: Firefly Books (U.S.) Inc., 1996.

Bryan, John E. *John E. Bryan on Bulbs*. New York, New York: Macmillan, 1994.

Coleman, Eliot. *The New Organic Grower's Four-Season Harvest*. White River Junction, Vermont: Chelsea Green Publishing Company, 1992.

Frieze, Charlotte, M. *The Zone Garden: A Surefire Guide to Gardening in Your Zone*. New York, New York: Simon & Schuster, 1997.

Green, Douglas. *Tender Roses for Tough Climates*. Shelburne, Vermont: Chapters Publishing, Ltd., 1997.

Hill, Lewis. *Cold-Climate Gardening*. Pownal, Vermont: Storey Communications, Inc., 1990.

Meyer, M. Hockenberry, D.B. White, and H. Pellet. *Ornamental Grasses for Cold Climates*. St. Paul, Minnesota: Minnesota Extension Service, University of Minnesota, 1995.

Mickel, John. *Ferns for American Gardens*. New York, New York: Macmillan Publishing Company, 1994.

Ogden, Samuel. *The New England Vegetable Garden*. Woodstock, Vermont: The Countryman Press, 1957.

Osborne, Robert. *Hardy Trees and Shrubs: A Guide to Disease-Resistant Varieties for the North*. Toronto, Canada: Key Porter Books Limited, 1996.

Snyder, Leon C. *Gardening in the Upper Midwest*. Minneapolis, Minnesota: University of Minnesota Press, 1985.

Snyder, Leon C. *Native Plants for Northern Gardens*. Minneapolis, Minnesota: University of Minnesota Press, 1991.

Taylor's Guide to Ornamental Grasses. Boston, Massachusetts: Houghton Mifflin Company, 1997

Taylor's Guide to Shrubs. Boston, Massachusetts: Houghton Mifflin Company, 1987.

Taylor's Guide to Vegetables. Boston, Massachusetts: Houghton Mifflin Company, 1987.

Taylor's Master Guide to Gardening. Boston, Massachusetts: Houghton Mifflin Company, 1994.

SOURCES

Tenenbaum, David. *Taylor's Weekend Gardening Guides: Backyard Building Projects*. Boston, Massachusetts: Houghton Mifflin Company.

Thomas, Charles B. *Taylor's Weekend Gardening Guides: Water Gardens*. Boston, Massachusetts: Houghton Mifflin Company, 1997.

Vick, Roger. *Gardening: Plains and Upper Midwest*. Golden, Colorado: Fulcrum Publishing, 1991.

Wilson, Jim. *Masters of the Victory Garden: Specialty Growers Share Their Techniques*. Boston, Massachusetts: Little, Brown and Company, 1990.

Wyman, Donald. *Trees for American Gardens*. New York, New York: Macmillan Publishing Company, 1990.

Zuzek, Kathy, Marcia Richards, Steve McNamara, and Harold Pellett. *Roses for the North: Performance of Shrub and Old Garden Roses at the Minnesota Landscape Arboretum*. St. Paul, Minnesota: Minnesota Agricultural Experiment Station, University of Minnesota, 1995.

Allen, Sterling & Lothrop, 191 US Rt. 1, Falmouth, ME 04105-1385 (207) 781-4142 (seed: vegetables, herbs, annuals, perennials)

Alpen Gardens, 173 Lawrence Lane, Kalispell, MT 59901 (406) 257-2540 (hardy dahlias)

Alpine Gardens, 12446 County Hwy F, Stitzer, WI 53825 (608) 822-6382 (hardy sedums and sepervivums)

Appalachian Gardens, Box 87, Waynesboro, PA 17268-0087 (888) 327-5483 (shrubs, trees, ornamental grasses, perennials, ground covers)

Kurt Bluemel, Inc., 2740 Green Lane, Baldwin, MD 21023 (410) 557-7229 (ornamental grasses)

Breck's, 6523 North Galena Road, Peoria, IL 61632 (800) 722-9069 (bulbs)

Busse Gardens, 5873 Oliver Avenue SW, Cokato, MN 55321-4229 (800) 544-3192 (perennials)

W. Atlee Burpee & Co., Warminster, PA 18974 (800) 888-1447 (annuals, perennials, bulbs, roses, vegetables, herbs)

The Cook's Garden, P.O. Box 535, Londonderry, VT 05148 (800) 457-9703 (vegetables, herbs, annuals, perennials)

Crystal Palace Perennials, P.O. Box 154, St. John, IN 46373 (219) 374-9419 (aquatic and marginal plants, ornamental grasses)

The Daffodil Mart, 30 Irene Street, Torrington, CT 06790-6668 (800) ALL-BULB (bulbs, perennials)

Gardener's Supply Company, 128 Intervale Road, Burlington, VT 05401-2850 (800) 955-3370 www.gardeners.com (row covers, gardening tools)

Hortico, Inc., 723 Robson Road, RR1, Waterdown, Ontario, Canada L0R 2HI (905) 689-6984 (roses)

Jackson and Perkins, P.O. Box 1028, Medford, OR 97501 (800) 292-4769 (perennials, roses, bulbs)

Johnny's Selected Seeds, 1 Foss Hill Road, RR1, Box 2580, Albion, ME 04910-9731 (207) 437-4301 (vegetables, herbs, flowers)

Limerock Ornamental Grasses, Inc., 70 Sawmill Road, Port Matilda, PA 16870 (814) 692-2272 (ornamental grasses)

Mike Lowe's Own-Root Roses, 6 Sheffield Road, Nashua, NH 03062 (roses)

McClure & Zimmerman, 108 West Winnebago Street, P.O. Box 368, Friesland, WI 53935-0368 (800) 883-6998 (bulbs)

Prairie Nursery, Westfield, WI 53964 (608) 296-3679 (wildflowers, native grasses)

The Roseraie at Bayfields, P.O. Box R, Waldboro, ME 04572-0919 (207) 832-6330 (roses)

Royal River Roses, 70 New Gloucester Road, North Yarmouth, ME 04097 (207) 829-5830 (roses)

John Scheepers, Inc., 23 Tulip Drive, Bantam, CT 06750 (860) 567-0838 (bulbs)

Shepherd's Garden Seeds, 30 Irene Street, Torrington, CT 06790-6658 (860) 482-3638 (vegetables, herbs, annuals, perennials)

Van Bourgondien, 245 Route 109, P.O. Box 1000, Babylon, NY 11702-9004 (800) 622-9959 (perennials, bulbs)

Andre Viette Farm and Nursery, Rt. 1, Box 16, Fisherville, VA 22939 (540) 943-2315 (perennials, ferns, ornamental grasses, flowering shrubs, daylilies, iris)

Wayside Gardens, Hodges, SC 29695-0001 (800) 845-1124 (perennials, bulbs, roses, ornamental grasses, shrubs)

Weston Nurseries, East Main Street (Rt. 135), P.O. Box 186, Hopkinton, MA 01748 (508) 435-3414 (perennials, roses, climbers, trees, shrubs)

White Flower Farm, P.O. Box 50, Litchfield, CT 06759-0050 (800) 503-9624 (perennials, bulbs, roses, vines, shrubs)

PHOTO CREDITS

David Cavagnaro: 2, 18, 21, 29, 31, 32, 35, 46, 50, 53, 58, 68, 69, 78, 81, 83, 101, 102, 105, 108

Gardener's Supply Company: 6 left, 6 right, 9, 10, 17

Marge Garfield: iii, 1, 12, 22, 49, 51, 66, 73, 77, 98

Johnny's Selected Seeds, Albion, Maine: 36, 39, 45

Mike Lowe: 88, 92, 93, 94, 97

Rick Mastelli: 24, 26, 62, 70, 87, 90

INDEX

Page numbers in italics refer to illustrations.

Titles available in the Taylor's Weekend Gardening Guides series:

Organic Pest and Disease Control
Safe and Easy Lawn Care
Window Boxes
Attracting Birds and Butterflies
Water Gardens
Easy, Practical Pruning
The Winter Garden
Backyard Building Projects
Indoor Gardens
Plants for Problem Places
Soil and Composting
Kitchen Gardens
Garden Paths
Easy Plant Propagation
Small Gardens
Fragrant Gardens
Cold Climate Gardening
The Cutting Garden
Cooking from the Garden

At your bookstore or by calling 1-800-225-3362